OSPREY
PUBLISHING

Ninja
AD 1460–1650

Stephen Turnbull • Illustrated by Wayne Reynolds

First published in Great Britain in 2003 by Osprey Publishing,
Elms Court, Chapel Way, Botley, Oxford OX2 9LP, United Kingdom.
Email: info@ospreypublishing.com

A CIP catalogue record for this book is available from the British Library

ISBN 1 84176 525 2

Editor: Tom Lowres
Design: Ken Vail Graphic Design
Index by Alan Rutter
Originated by The Electronic Page Company, Cwmbran, UK
Printed in China through World Print Ltd.

04 05 06 07   10 9 8 7 6 5 4 3 2

FOR A CATALOGUE OF ALL BOOKS PUBLISHED BY OSPREY, MILITARY AND
AVIATION, PLEASE CONTACT:

Osprey Direct UK, PO Box 140, Wellingborough, Northants, NN8 2FA, UK
E-mail: info@ospreydirect.co.uk

Osprey Direct USA, c/o MBI Publishing, P.O. Box 1, 729 Prospect Ave,
Osceola, WI 54020, USA
E-mail: info@ospreydirectusa.com

www.ospreypublishing.com

Author's dedication

For our nephew, Jonathan Charles Turnbull, on his 21st birthday.

Author's note

In this search for the maximum authenticity among a maze of romantic
accretions I would like to acknowledge the help received in the preparation of
this book by the staff of the ninja museums of Iga-Ueno, Koga and Togakure.
The illustrations have been greatly enhanced by the members of the ninja re-
enactment group of Iga-Ueno, who kindly and patiently posed for photographs.
I would particularly like to thank my wife for her usual endeavours in picture
research and administration.

Editor's note

All pictures from the author's collection unless stated.

Artist's note

Readers may care to note that the original paintings from which the colour
plates in this book were prepared are available for private sale. All reproduction
copyright whatsoever is retained by the Publishers. All enquiries should be
addressed to:

Wayne Reynolds,
20 Woodside Place,
Burley,
Leeds,
LS4 SQU

The Publishers regret that they can enter into no correspondence upon this
matter.

CONTENTS

NINJA AD 1460–1650

INTRODUCTION: THE ELUSIVE NINJA

Few military organisations in world history are so familiar yet so misunderstood as Japan's ninja, so to write a Warriors book on the topic provides a unique challenge. Ninja certainly existed, but so much myth and exaggeration has grown up around the undoubted historical core of the subject that writing a book such as this could be almost as daunting a prospect as producing a Warriors volume on the outlaws of Robin Hood. To resolve the matter I have decided to 'play it straight'. Any references to ninja that could fly will be identified as the myths they are. Quotations from written accounts of ninja exploits will be confined to chronicles that are respected for their accuracy. Descriptions of items of ninja equipment will be confined to implements illustrated in old 'ninja manuals' such as the 17th-century *Bansen Shukai*, or preserved in one of Japan's several (and remarkably underplayed) ninja museums. The reader will therefore find collapsible ladders, secret explosives and hidden staircases, but will have to look elsewhere for human cannonballs and ninja submarines.

This woodblock print by Yoshitoshi is a fine print of a ninja assassination. The traditional details associated with ninja are perfectly depicted. The ninja is attempting to murder Oda Nobunaga in 1573. He tried to sneak into Nobunaga's castle of Azuchi to stab Nobunaga while he was asleep in his bedroom, but was discovered and captured by two of the guards. He then committed suicide, and his body was displayed in the local market place to discourage any other would-be killers.

NINJA – JAPAN'S SECRET WARRIORS

For any military historian the ninja remains one of the most fascinating mysteries of Japanese samurai warfare. The word *ninja* or its alternative reading *shinobi* crops up again and again in historical accounts in the context of secret intelligence gathering or assassinations carried out by martial-arts experts. Many opportune deaths may possibly be credited to ninja activities, but as they were so secret it is impossible to prove either way. The ways of the ninja were therefore an unavoidable part of samurai warfare, and no samurai could ignore the secret threat they posed, which could ruin all his carefully laid plans. As a result ninja were both used and feared, although they were almost invariably despised because of the contrast their ways presented to the samurai code of behaviour. This may be partly due to the fact that many ninja had their origins in the lower social classes, and that their secretive and underhand methods were the exact opposite of the ideals of the noble samurai facing squarely on to his enemy.

This paradox, that ninja were beneath contempt and yet indispensable, is a theme running through the whole history of ninja warfare. It is also fascinating to note that the popular extension of the image of the ninja to a superhuman that could fly and perform magic also has a surprisingly long history in Japan. Such stories were being told as early as the beginning of the 17th century, when many of the historical accounts became mixed up with other legends.

The roots of the ninja

Secret operations, from guerrilla warfare to the murder of prominent rivals, are topics that may be found throughout Japanese history, but it is only from about the mid-15th century onwards that we find references to such activities being carried out by specially trained individuals who belonged to organisations dedicated to this type of warfare. Much of the activity is focused around the Iga and Koga areas of central Japan, so this location and time period will provide the major setting for this book.

The traditional view of the ninja as a secret, superlative, black-coated spy and assassin derives from two different roots. The first is the area of undercover work, of espionage and intelligence gathering (and even assassination) that is indispensable to the waging of war. The second is the use of mercenaries, whereby the leaders of military operations pay outsiders to fight for them. In Japan these two elements came together to produce the ninja and, curiously enough, the ninja provide almost the only example of mercenaries being used in Japanese warfare. Part of the reason for this was that secret operations were the antithesis of the samurai ideal. A *daimyo* (warlord) would not wish to have his brave and noble samurai's reputations soiled by carrying out

Ninja with sword. A member of the Iga-Ueno ninja re-enactment society poses for the camera during the 2002 Ninja Festival.

such despicable acts. Instead he paid others to do them. It was an unusual but highly valued service, and the Japanese historian Watatani sums up the situation as follows:

> So-called ninjutsu techniques, in short are the skills of shinobi-no-jutsu and shinobi-jutsu, which have the aims of ensuring that one's opponent does not know of one's existence, and for which there was special training. During the Sengoku Period such techniques were used on campaign, and included sekko (spy) and kancho (espionage) techniques and skills.

The term *shinobi* is merely the alternative reading of the character *nin*; hence *shinobi no mono* rather than *ninja*. But ninja trips more readily off a Western tongue, and has therefore become the popular term.

The ancestors of the ninja

As undercover operations are fundamental to the conduct of war in any culture, it is not surprising to read of such techniques being used throughout Japan's own turbulent history, but the first written account confirms that even at that early stage such activities were somehow questionable, even when they produced results. In *Shomonki*, the *gunkimono* (war tale) that deals with the life of Taira Masakado and was probably completed shortly after his death in AD940, we read:

> Over forty of the enemy were killed on that day, and only a handful managed to escape with their lives. Those who were able to survive the fighting fled in all directions, blessed by Heaven's good fortune. As for Yoshikane's spy Koharumaru, Heaven soon visited its punishment upon him; his misdeeds were found out, and he was captured and killed.

Spying was the classic ninja role, so we may note here the first written confirmation that such activities were perceived as contrary to samurai behaviour. Like *Shomonki*, the two greatest gunkimono, *Hogen Monogatari* and *Heike Monogatari*, were written for an aristocratic audience who wished to hear of the glorious deeds of their ancestors. The activities of the common foot soldiers, who outnumbered the mounted samurai by 20 to one in the armies of

Ninja with a *shinobi-gama* (kusari-gama). Combination weapons involving sickles were a popular choice for ninja.

the time, are almost totally ignored, so it is not surprising that stories of ignoble undercover acts are conspicuous by their absence. The one exception is the story that begins *Heike Monogatari*, when Taira Tadamori thwarts an attempt to assassinate him by using the sort of trick later attributed to skilled ninja. Being warned beforehand that rivals in the Court intended his death:

... he provided himself with a long dagger which he put on under his long court dress, and turning aside to a dimly lit place, slowly drew the blade, and passed it through the hair of his head so that it gleamed afar with an icy sheen, causing all to stare open-eyed.

The bringing of weapons within the presence of the emperor was a serious offence, and Tadamori was ordered to give an account of himself, whereupon he showed that the knife was a dummy, but it had frightened off the assassin.

We hear nothing more of ninja-like activities during the decisive Gempei War of 1180–85. Instead it was conventional samurai warfare that established Japan's first shogunate, the rule by a shogun (military dictator). The first family of shoguns was the Minamoto, and even though the Hojo family usurped them, the mechanism of military government helped ensure a century and a half of comparative peace in Japan.

Ninja activities in the 14th century

Undercover operations may have been contrary to the samurai ideal, but when fighting began again in Japan they had to be used if victory was to be gained. During the 14th century a war broke out when Emperor Go-Daigo tried to regain the power that had been taken away from the imperial line by the shogun. The result was that Japan ended up with two rival emperors, and *Taiheiki*, the chronicle of the Nanbokucho Wars (the 'Wars between the Courts'), tells how ninja were involved in the destruction by fire of a fortress called Hachiman-yama:

> ... the fall of this castle would benefit the enemies of the Southern Court, and in Kyoto there were enemies from the northern provinces who remembered the approach through the valley. One night, under the cover of rain and wind, Hachiman-yama was approached by a highly skilled shinobi who set fire to the temple.

Ninja jumping. A ninja re-enactor demonstrates the jumping technique that fostered the belief that the ninja could fly.

Elsewhere we read another account of a similar secret raid on a fortified place, a speciality that the ninja were to make their own: 'In 1367 ... on the 11th day of the same month Tadaoka Rokugoro Saemon cut down a shinobi who had entered Ototsu castle.'

The *Taiheiki* also contains the earliest account of a ninja-like assassination. The assassin was not a professional ninja, but young Kumawaka, the 13-year-old son of a certain Lord Suketomo, who had been sent into exile for his part in the conspiracy of Go-Daigo. Suketomo had been placed in the custody of the lay monk Homma Saburo, who had him executed. Kumawaka swore revenge on Homma Saburo, and for someone who was not a professional assassin his preparations were

The komuso, flute-playing Zen mendicants, provided a useful disguise for a ninja as they were able to roam the country at will, their identity disguised beneath the curious 'wastepaper basket' hat. These komuso, however, are the genuine article, photographed in Yura (Wakayama Prefecture) during the midnight Bon Festival in August 1997.

commendably thorough. He first feigned illness so as not to be sent back to Kyoto with his father's mortal remains, and the apparent affliction also ensured for him a place within Homma Saburo's house.

He chose well his moment to strike. It was a night of violent rain and wind, and the guards on duty were sleeping in their quarters beyond the courtyard. Homma Saburo had actually changed his sleeping room, but Kumawaka found it out, and was about to rush upon him when he remembered that he had not actually got a sword of his own, a strange omission for an assassin. Realising that he would have to do the deed with Saburo's own sword, he was concerned that the light burning in the room would awaken him when Kumawaka attempted to draw it from its scabbard. The means he used to prevent this happening would have done credit to any ninja:

> … gazing towards the lamp he beheld a multitude of moths clinging to the clear sliding doors, the season being summer. Thereupon he set a door ajar, so that the insects entered in swarms, quickly putting out the light.

Kumawaka slowly drew Saburo's sword. He held the point of the blade to his victim's chest, kicked the pillow away and drove the sword into his body. Kumawaka's subsequent escape to safety is also in true ninja style:

> He thought to jump across the moat, yet in no wise might he do it, for it was six yards wide and more than ten feet deep. But then he climbed nimbly to the top of a black bamboo growing above the water, saying, 'I will cross by making a bridge of this.' And the tip thereof bent down to the other side, so that he crossed over easily.

Ninja in the age of war

The pivotal event in samurai history was the Onin War, which lasted from 1467 until 1477. It began over a succession dispute for the shogunate within the ruling Ashikaga family. It was a war that was fought with fire and starvation as much as with sword and bow, and it devastated both the capital city of Kyoto and the prestige of the shogun. The fighting quickly spread to the provinces and ushered in a period of a century and a half of war called the Sengoku Jidai – the Age of Warring States. The rival warlords called themselves *daimyo*, 'great names', and ninja were among the devices by which their wars were waged. For example, in the *Chugoku chiranki*, which deals with the fighting in western Japan, we read: 'The Amako were encamped on Aoyama Mitsukayama, and shinobi soldiers were sent from the Mori side, who cut their way through the enemy army on the mountain.'

The various uses to which shinobi or ninja were put during the Sengoku period are noted in the chronicles as *kancho* (spies) in enemy provinces, and in times of war *teisatsu* (scouts), *kisho* (surprise attackers), and *koran* (agitators). We must, however, distinguish between the expert ninja, who passed their traditions on to their descendants, of which the Iga ninja are the best example, and others who were no more than brigands hired temporarily as spies or ordinary samurai given a secret operation.

Ninja were often mistrusted by their own allies, and their actions were sometimes perceived as no more than theft or revenge disguised as important operations. However, when taken along as hired mercenaries within an army, ninja were treated with respect, as related in *Ou Eikei Gunki*, in the section dealing with the fall of Hataya castle in 1600:

The famous Myoryuji or Ninjadera (ninja temple) in Kanazawa (Ishikawa Prefecture) is one of the best of the very few authentic 'ninja-proofed' buildings to have survived. This is a view of the shoji staircase. The vertical sections of the tread are of translucent paper, enabling a spear thrust to be delivered against any unwelcome caller.

Within Hataya castle there was a glorious shinobi whose skill was renowned, and one night he entered the enemy camp secretly. He took the flag from Naoe Kanetsugu's guard Temmago Zamon and returned and stood it on a high place on the front gate of the castle.

The ninja of Iga and Koga

The most celebrated 'professional' ninja were of course the mercenaries of Iga and Koga, whose lives and activities will fill most of this book. They were hired and used by rival daimyo from about 1485 to 1581, when a dramatic attack on their province curtailed their activities. So rapid and devastating was this onslaught that there was no time for the inhabitants to deploy ninja techniques. Instead they fought like ordinary samurai in bloody pitched battles. The invasion of Iga was carried out by the daimyo Oda Nobunaga, who was the first of the three 'super-daimyo' who eventually reunited Japan.

Interior view of the Ninjadera in Kanazawa, which formed part of the outer defence works for Kanazawa castle, the seat of the Maeda daimyo.

The survivors of the 1581 invasion fled to other provinces. Some headed for the remote mountains of Kii, but others made it to nearby Mikawa, where they were well treated by Tokugawa Ieyasu, who was destined to become the last of the three unifiers and who revived the shogunate in 1603. Back in 1581 he was just another daimyo, but from this time onwards all the activities of the ninja of Iga and Koga were conducted on behalf of the Tokugawa family, and their mercenary days were over. Tokugawa Ieyasu was an astute politician, and surely nothing illustrates his foresight better than the fact that he took Japan's finest ninja into his service.

Their refuge with the Tokugawa was the beginning of a long and beneficial association with the future shogun, and the inhabitants of Iga were able to repay the kindness very soon. In 1582 Oda Nobunaga was murdered by Akechi Mitsuhide, who then set himself up as shogun and began to hunt down any rivals. Tokugawa Ieyasu was visiting Sakai when the coup occurred. Having only a handful of personal retainers with him, he was faced with the difficult prospect of getting back to Mikawa by sea or land without being intercepted by the Akechi samurai. The overland route lay via Iga, so with the help of local supporters Ieyasu set off. The *Mikawa Go Fudoki* continues the story:

> From here on it was mountain roads and precipices as far as Shigaraki, with many mountain bandits. Yamaoka and Hattori accompanied them, defying mountain bandits and yamabushi alike. ... Hattori Sadanobu was praised for the great extent of his loyalty, and on leaving he was presented with a wakizashi [short sword] forged by Kunitsugu. ... Yamaoka, father and son, took their leave beyond the Tomi pass on the Iga border.

Thus, by a combination of friendly guides they made it to the Iga border. Here more allies took over:

A view of the successive roofs of the Ninjadera in Kanazawa.

> Hattori Hanzo Masashige was an Iga man. Sent on by Tadakatsu, he went ahead as guide to the roads of Iga. The previous year, when Lord Oda had persecuted Iga, he had ordered, 'The samurai of the province must all be killed.' Because of this people fled to the Tokugawa territories of Mikawa and Totomi, where it was ordered that they be shown kindness and consideration. Consequently their relatives were able to pay them back for this kindness. Beginning with Tsuge Sannojo Kiyohiro and his son, 2 or 300 men of Tsuge village, and over 100 Koga samurai under Shima Okashi no suke and others … came to serve him … and they passed through the middle of the mountains that were the dens of mountain bandits.

The serious nature of the perils Ieyasu faced is illustrated by the fate of his retainer Anayama Baisetsu, who took a different route back to Mikawa and was murdered along the way. There is also a story in connection with Ieyasu's escape that is almost too good a ninja tale to be false! Akechi's men, who had been ordered to be on the lookout for him, searched the ship in which Ieyasu fled from Ise. Ieyasu was hidden under the cargo in the hold. The soldiers began thrusting their long-bladed spears into the cargo to find anyone concealed therein. One of

Hattori Hanzo, the leader of the ninja of Iga and a samurai general in his own right under Tokugawa Ieyasu, is buried in this grave in the grounds of the Seinenji temple in Tokyo. Hanzo's spear is preserved inside the temple.

the spearblades cut his leg, but Ieyasu responded coolly by taking the head towel from his forehead and quickly wiping the blade clean of blood before it was withdrawn.

Serving the shogun

Oda Nobunaga's murder was avenged by the second of the unifiers, Toyotomi Hideyoshi, who marched his army against Kyoto and destroyed Akechi Mitsuhide at the battle of Yamazaki. From this time on Hideyoshi went from strength to strength, and over the next 20 years conquered the whole of Japan. When he defeated the Hojo in 1590 he gave Tokugawa Ieyasu their territories as a reward. Ieyasu chose not to base himself at the Hojo's main fortress of Odawara but further east in the small town of Edo. It was a successful move, as Edo is now called Tokyo, and what is now the palace of the emperor of Japan was Ieyasu's own Edo castle, guarded by the men of Iga and Koga.

The Iga detachment at Edo was under the command of the man who appears in popular works as the most famous ninja of all, Hattori Hanzo Masashige, who had acted as a guide through Iga. Hanzo was born in 1541, the son of Hattori Yasunaga, a hereditary retainer of the Tokugawa. He fought his first battle at the age of 16 in the form of a night attack on the castle of Udo in 1557, and went on to serve with distinction at the battles of Anegawa (1570) and Mikata ga Hara (1572). His nickname was 'Devil Hanzo'. He died in 1596, aged 55, and was succeeded by his son, Hattori Masanari.

The later wars in which ninja were involved on behalf of the Tokugawa will be described in the section 'Ninja at war'. From 1638 onwards Japan was at peace, and military skills declined, yet during this time the myth of the ninja as we know it today began to grow, until a mixture of historical accounts and legends produced the 'superman' ninja who could fly in the air.

RECRUITMENT AND TRAINING

Ninja recruitment

From the mid-15th century onwards, certain samurai families began to develop particular skills in intelligence gathering, undercover warfare and assassination. These were the ninja families. Like so many other martial-arts traditions in Japan, their skills and traditions were passed on from father to son, or more usually from *sensei* (master) to chosen pupil,

12

who may not always have been a relative. In a real sense, therefore, ninja were born, not made, and the expression 'recruitment' refers only to the negotiations made between daimyo and the ninja leader for the use of his men's services.

However, when Tokugawa Ieyasu took the men of Iga and Koga under his personal wing in 1581, the source of supply dried up, and we begin to see other daimyo training and using their own home-grown ninja. Strangely enough, this was not officially forbidden, and in 1649, in the shogunate's laws for military service, we read that only those daimyo with incomes of 10,000 koku and above were allowed to have shinobi in their armies.

The school of ninjutsu called the Nakagawa-ryu, which served the daimyu Tsugaru in Mutsu Province in the mid-17th century, provides a good example of the recruitment and training process. The founder of the school was a samurai called Nakagawa Shoshunjin, an expert in ninjutsu. The most fascinating account of his life is the *Okufuji monogatari*, which says that 'he could change into a rat or a spider, and transform himself into birds and animals' – an early illustration of the magical powers traditionally attributed to ninja.

A ninja crossing a castle moat using a hooked rope is the earliest known illustration of the traditional image of the ninja in action. It dates from 1801.

In reality Shoshunjin had the command of a group of ten young samurai whom he trained to practise ninjutsu, and forbade anyone else from coming near the place where they exercised, which was at the southern corner of the castle and called Ishibayashi. Shoshunjin called the group the *Hayamichi no mono* ('the short-cut people') and its numbers soon increased to 20. Since the duties of the group members were to act as spies or secret agents, they were put into operation entirely on the word of the daimyo, and their training was kept strictly secret.

Ninja selection

There is a splendid story about Nakagawa Shoshunjin's first visit to the Tsugaru mansion to be interviewed by Tsugaru Gemban, a *karo* (senior retainer) of the Tsugaru. Tsugaru Gemban challenged Shoshunjin to prove his ninja abilities by stealing the pillow from under his head while he lay sleeping. That night Gemban lay down on his futon, and as time passed he heard the pitter-patter of a passing shower beginning to fall outside the house. He carefully avoided letting his head move from the pillow, until he suddenly felt rain falling on to his face. He raised his eyes, and quickly noticed that the ceiling was leaking. In spite of himself his head moved off the pillow at an angle. When he lowered his head once again the pillow was missing, and as he turned his head in surprise he saw Shoshunjin standing beside him, grinning broadly, and with the pillow in his hands!

Ninja in a narrow corridor. This posed shot, kindly supplied by the Department of Tourism of Iga-Ueno City, depicts perfectly the classic image of the ninja approaching his prey.

Unfortunately, the story is probably not authentic, as similar versions are told of other ninja employed by daimyo. For example, Mori Motonari's general Sugiwara Harima-no-kami used a ninja, who, according to legend, was asked to steal a sword from his master's bedside, and a certain Kato Dansai was asked to steal a naginata from beside the bed of Naoe Yamashiro-no-kami of the Uesugi family. Nevertheless, it illustrates the respect that the daimyo had for ninja skills, and the need to hire someone who could be trusted.

Ninja training

We may certainly envisage the ninja of Iga and Koga being trained for their future roles as soon as they could walk. The ninja leaders of the province were minor landowners, and, in common with all daimyo of any size, great emphasis was laid on family connections and hereditary loyalty. Any boy born into a conventional samurai family would grow up expecting to be a warrior, and many hours of his childhood would be spent learning the martial arts. Skills with the famous samurai sword, the spear, bow and, later in ninja history, guns would be most important. A young samurai would also be expected to ride well and to swim.

For a young ninja, of course, the curriculum would be more extensive. He would also have to learn about such matters as explosives and the blending of poisons, and become an expert in fieldcraft and survival. This would include such 'ninja lore' as how to purify water and how to cook rice in camp by wrapping it in a wet cloth and burying it underneath a campfire.

He would have to be superbly physically fit to enable him to scale the walls of castles and become an expert in martial arts, including unarmed grappling techniques. We may therefore envisage the fledgling ninja being trained from an early age in all these skills. He would also have to know how to draw a map and would have a great advantage if he could read and write. If he was to adopt the disguises of other professions, he would need an in-depth knowledge of them to be convincing.

Belief and belonging

At a psychological level the young ninja would need to develop a detachment from death and the fear of dying that was even more complete than that customarily expected of ordinary samurai, who were presented with the ideal of serving their masters with unflinching zeal to the very end. 'The way of the samurai,' wrote a famous warrior, 'is found in death', and how much more it was in the way of the ninja. There was also the chilling samurai tradition of ritual suicide, whereby, in situations of certain defeat, any disgrace could be wiped away by the act of *hara kiri* that released one's spirit.

The ninja's concept of his own fate was therefore a more intense version of the samurai worldview. The major difference in attitude that would be inculcated in the ninja, as distinct from the samurai, was the complete acceptance of the knife in the dark as a legitimate activity. This was contrary to so much of the samurai tradition that relied on stories of noble warriors who fought in an ideal and often idealised way. The accepted samurai code involved first of all being very visible, so that both friends and enemies recognised who it was that won the supreme distinction of being the first to go into battle or the first to scale a castle wall during an assault. To make identification easier a samurai wore a flag on the back of his suit of armour. Once engaged in battle, the ideal outcome was for the samurai to locate a worthy opponent and take his head. This trophy would be presented to the daimyo, who would note the names of both victor and victim, and reward his loyal follower accordingly.

How different it was for a ninja. Dressed in black and with no flag to identify him, his role in a siege would be to enter the castle days before the assault and lie low until emerging to cause mayhem by setting fire to towers, killing guards or even assassinating the commander. His job done, the ninja would withdraw into anonymity and let the first samurai in the assault party receive all the glory. It was an attitude totally different from the rest of samurai warfare, and carried the additional opprobrium that the noble samurai, who depended upon the ninja's activities for his own achievements, officially despised the ninja for behaving in such an underhand way.

Ninja mail armour. This ensemble from the Arashiyama Historical Museum in Kyoto shows a simple suit of armour that could have been worn under a ninja's costume.

APPEARANCE AND EQUIPMENT

Men in black

The traditional ninja garb of a full black costume is so well known that it is usually taken for granted, but there are in fact no authentic written accounts where ninja are actually described as being dressed in black. Usually they appear to have disguised themselves to blend in with the enemy. As the *Buke Meimokusho* relates:

Ninja lightweight armour. This item from the Arashiyama Historical Museum in Kyoto is a suit of armour made from metal plates sewn on to a cloth backing. It could have been worn under a ninja's costume.

They travelled in disguise to other territories to judge the situation of the enemy, they would inveigle their way into the midst of the enemy to discover gaps, and enter enemy castles to set them on fire, and carried out assassinations, arriving in secret.

The earliest pictorial reference to a ninja in black is a book illustration of 1801, which shows a ninja climbing into a castle wearing what everyone would immediately recognise as a ninja costume. However, it could simply be that it is pictures like these that have given us our image of the ninja rather than vice-versa. It is a long-standing artistic convention in Japan, seen today in the Bunraku puppet theatre, that to dress a character in black is to indicate to the viewer that he cannot see that person. To depict a silent assassin in an identical way in a picture would therefore be perfectly natural and understandable to the contemporary Japanese viewer, and need not imply that the resulting illustration is in any way an actual portrait of a ninja.

Nevertheless, it is obvious that if a ninja was to perform the role most often noted for him, that of entering a castle in secret by night, then a head-to-foot costume of black would be the most sensible thing to wear. We may therefore safely conclude that in this situation at least the traditional black costume was authentic, although some authorities maintain that the black was tinged with a little red so that bloodstains would not show.

An old book illustration showing samurai practising their throwing of shuriken, the favourite ninja weapon. As well as the familiar 'ninja stars', short knives were also used.

The ninja costume

The ninja costume was simple but very well designed for its purpose. The jacket was not unlike the jacket worn for judo or karate, having no ties. So that nothing would catch on any protrusions when climbing a wall, the 'tails' of the jacket were tucked inside the trousers. These were like the trousers commonly worn by samurai when riding a horse. They were quite narrow and tied below the knee. Over the calves would be worn cloth gaiters, again very similar to standard samurai equipment, while on the feet would be black *tabi*, the classic Japanese socks with a separate compartment for the big toe, and reinforced soles. *Waraji* (straw sandals) would

complete the ninja's footwear. A shirt with close-fitting arms also seems to have been worn according to most illustrations, and the whole ensemble was pulled tightly together round the waist by a long black belt. The biggest difference from a samurai's costume, however, was to be found above the neck, because the ninja's head was wrapped in an all-enveloping cowl, with only the face above the mouth, or even only the eye slits visible.

Several museums in Japan have examples of lightweight body armour that could be worn under the ninja costume. The construction was that of a heavy cloth backing on to which were sewn small lacquered metal plates joined by thin sections of ring mail. Reinforced hoods, not unlike the ninja cowl, were made of similar material. As the *ashigaru* (foot soldiers) in a samurai army wore very different types of armour, it is not unreasonable to associate these simple body armours with ninja. Standard samurai *kote* (sleeve armour) and *suneate* (shin guards) would also have provided extra protection for very little additional weight.

Ninja disguises

The use of disguise is frequently mentioned in the chronicles, and different disguises suited different situations. If the ninja was required to travel widely round an enemy's territory observing the layout of troops and the defensive features of his castles, what better cover could there be but to assume the role of a *komuso*, the sect of Zen monks who played the flute and wore enormous baskets over their heads? They would be seen on the highways and byways, playing music and begging. The itinerant *yamabushi* (the mountain monks) were also frequently seen on Japanese roads, and this was a better disguise to adopt when the mission was to deliver a message in private to a friendly ally, because yamabushi were invited into people's homes to say prayers and give blessings. Even a simple Buddhist monk sent out begging, his face partly concealed by a large sedge hat, might be a ninja. Strolling players such as *sarugaku* dancers and puppeteers might provide cover for spying activities in a daimyo's castle town. They would no doubt be searched for weapons if they were invited to give a performance inside a castle, but the mere act of entering a castle and making one's way through the maze of interlocking walls and gates to the daimyo's private apartments would yield much valuable intelligence for a rival.

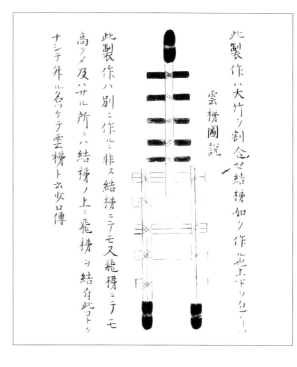

This illustration from *Bansen Shukai*, the manual of ninja lore published in 1683, shows a ladder with a hinged section. The ladder is light in weight.

Standard ninja equipment

The most important ninja weapon was his sword. This was the standard Japanese fighting sword or *katana*, renowned for its strength and sharpness. The Japanese sword was also designed to be flexible, so that it could act as both sword and shield when the samurai parried a rival's blow and then delivered a deadly cut of his own. This factor would have been very important for the lightly armed ninja. Both the length and curve of katana blades varied considerably, and for convenience the ninja would choose a blade that was shorter and straighter than usual. To make climbing easier, the sword would not be thrust through the belt, as was usual for a samurai out of armour, but would be carried over the shoulder with the blade edge up and the handle near the left ear.

One other way of carrying a sword must be mentioned. This arose from the ninja technique of exploring a potentially dangerous dark place such as a castle's corridors. The ninja would balance the sword's scabbard out in front on the tip of the sword blade, with the scabbard's suspensory cords gripped firmly between his teeth. This extended the ninja's range of feel by a good six feet, and if the scabbard end encountered an enemy, the ninja would let it fall and lunge forward in the precise direction of the assailant. A sword could also be used in

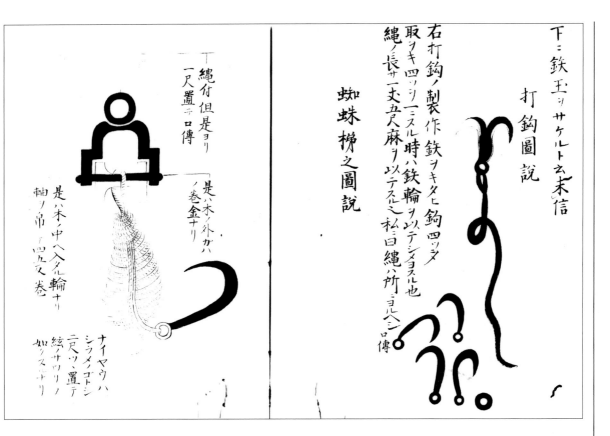

climbing a wall, because the strong iron *tsuba* (sword-guard) could provide a step if the sword was leant against the wall. The ninja would loop the end of the suspensory cord round his foot so that he could pull his sword up when he had climbed the wall.

Needless to say, the ninja would have had an array of weapons secreted about his person. A simple-looking Japanese folding fan might well conceal a knife blade. Heavy iron knuckle-dusters called *tekagi* are also known. Another fairly standard piece of ninja equipment was a hooked rope for climbing. This consisted of a three- or four-pronged grapnel attached to a coil of thin but very strong rope. It was most conveniently carried hanging from the belt. A utility bag might also be suspended from the belt, and this could contain small throwing weapons such as knives or the well-known *shuriken* (ninja stars) that were flung with a spinning motion. *Tetsu bishi* (caltrops) could also be carried. These consisted of iron spikes arranged in the shape of a tetrahedron so that one spike was always protruding upwards. As samurai wore thin-soled footwear, tetsu bishi could be very effective in slowing down pursuers. Poisons and their antidotes and emergency food supplies might also find their way into the utility bag when appropriate. Other pieces of standard ninja equipment are illustrated in Plate A.

Specialised ninja equipment

There was also a weird and wonderful array of specialised weapons and devices that ninja could use in appropriate circumstances. Many of these are drawn and described in *Bansen Shukai*, the ninja manual of the 17th century from which some of the accompanying illustrations

Hooks and ropes are shown in this illustration from *Bansen Shukai*. A hooked rope was a vital piece of ninja equipment.

are taken. We will deal first with devices to assist climbing into a castle – a very common ninja activity.

Let us consider the typical ninja attacking a castle in secret by night. First, he has to cross the ditch or moat. He could always swim, and even ordinary samurai were expected to be so skilled at swimming that they could use their weapons while treading water. But if explosives were involved in the ninja's plans then he could not risk getting the powder wet. He might therefore use his hooked rope to cross the moat hand-over-hand, but if the moat was wide a safer alternative might be to paddle across using some form of flotation device. The best known of these was the *mizugumo*, the wooden water shoes illustrated in *Bansen Shukai*, which look very unstable. *Bansen Shukai* also shows a prefabricated boat. Alternatively, if the ninja were operating as a group, one man could swim the moat and then help his comrades rig up the simple rope ladder shown in the accompanying picture.

The castle wall now had to be climbed, and in many cases the deeply curved stone walls with many gaps allowed the ninja to climb up without difficulty, but mechanical devices would sometimes be used. The standard hooked rope has already been mentioned, but for more difficult ascents some form of portable ladder was needed. The simplest was a straightforward rope ladder with strong wooden rungs and a stout hook at the top. An ingenious version of this consisted of a series of short bamboo sections. A rope was threaded through each section, alternating between pieces threaded across the middle and through their whole length. A hook was attached to the top, and when the whole length of the rope was pulled tight and secured the result was a lightweight if flimsy ladder. Other help might be provided for the feet by means of spiked climbing devices rather like crampons.

Having surmounted the stone base the ninja was faced with the white plaster walls that lay on top. Some were simple outer walls pierced by arrow and gun ports, others were made up of elaborate superstructures and towers. As there would be a considerable overhang because of the tiled protective surface on top of the white wall, the ninja might decide to cut his way into the defended position. Here the construction of the walls came most admirably to his assistance. They were made on a wattle and daub core and plastered over, so a ninja would use a *kunai*, which looked like a cross between a broad bladed knife and a paint scraper. By gouging and cutting, the ninja could rapidly carve out a hole large enough for him to climb through.

Many of the buildings within the walls of a Japanese castle were made of wood. In some cases these would include the daimyo's *yashiki* (mansion), which was often a palatial structure built in addition to the keep and used for entertaining visitors. It would be heavily guarded.

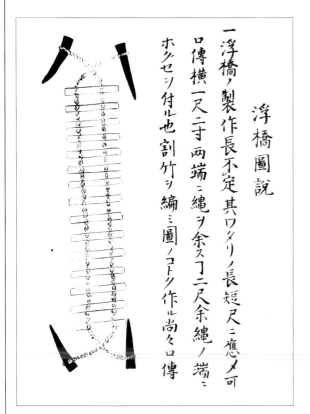

A rope ladder with wooden slats, designed to be affixed across a gap for others to cross, appears in this illustration from *Bansen Shukai*.

Portable listening devices called *saoto hikigane*, which acted like ear trumpets, enabled the ninja to listen in to conversations and ascertain the movements of guards. For a ninja to enter such a wooden building unseen he would have had to use some form of saw. Several types are illustrated in the ninja manuals. The *hamagari*, for example, was a long thin saw with many very sharp teeth mounted on a folding iron shaft like a penknife. Alternatively, using two devices in succession, the ninja could open small gaps between the planking. The first was like a two-pronged iron fork, which would enlarge the gap slightly by twisting, making a space just large enough for a thin leaf-shaped saw with small teeth to be inserted. It could even be used to crack the wood, but this would create a sound that might give the ninja away.

Ninja also had to be fully conversant with firearms and explosives technology. The matchlock arquebus, introduced to Japan in 1543, was too clumsy to be considered a ninja weapon except when it was used as a sniper's firearm. Matchlock pistols could more easily be carried by a ninja, but the ideally suited wheel-lock pistol arrived too late in Japan for it to be used in war. In addition the ninja had a huge range of mainly Chinese explosive devices at his disposal. There were two main types. The

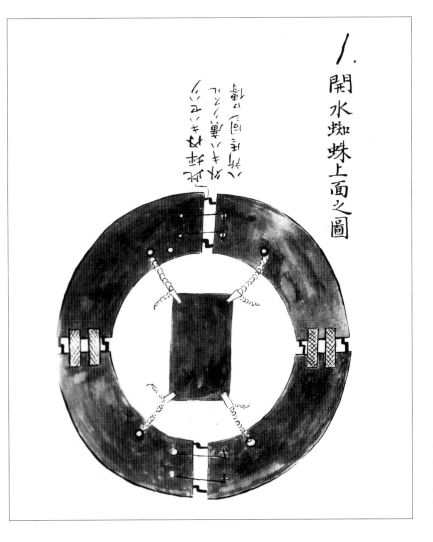

This illustration from *Bansen Shukai* is of the famous (and notorious!) water spider. One was supposed to have been worn on each foot to allow the ninja to cross water.

first were soft-cased bombs built round a paper or wicker carton and designed to release smoke or poison gas, or to alarm an enemy by its thunderclap explosion. Fragments of iron, broken pottery or dried human faeces could be included to make them into anti-personnel devices. The second type were hard-cased bombs, either of pottery or iron. The latter could produce fearful wounds like a fragmentation bomb, and large models would have had sufficient force to blow a hole in a castle's plaster walls. Small versions could be thrown by hand, making them effectively hand grenades. Ignition was provided from a tinderbox or a smouldering cord kept in a weatherproof lacquered container.

A ninja would also be expected to be a sharpshooter with a bow and arrow, and there were small versions of ninja bows that could be carried more easily. Ninja also made good use of the martial-arts weapons that were derived from agricultural implements, such as the *kusarigama*, the combination of a sickle and a chain. The chain had a weight on the end and could be flung to halt a pursuer. The attacker would then drag him off his feet and kill him with the sickle blade. The ninja version had a smaller but very sharp blade kept in a scabbard when not in use. It was called a *shinobigama*. For other illustrations of specialised ninja equipment and weapons see Plate A and B.

Ninja techniques
Ninja relied on more than just clever gadgets for entering defended places. Teamwork and co-operation were also essential, and well-practised acrobatic skills may well have given rise to the myths of ninja being able to fly. For example, there were two-, three- and four-man techniques for climbing over a wall. In the first type one ninja would run forward with his comrade on his shoulders. He would then leap from this elevated position. Two men could assist a third to 'fly' over a wall by giving him a powerful leg up. Four might construct a human pyramid.

Other ninja might use one of the foot soldier's pike-like long spears and pole-vault over a gap. It may even be the case that ninja were lifted off the ground using kites to spy on an enemy castle or

The special *geta* (clogs) for use with the water spider, from an illustration in *Bansen Shukai*.

水掻ノ圖

一 水掻ノ製作カメハ〱ノ木履ノ如クシテ裏ニ口ク石有

上ニ八ナ緒シ付ハシナリ

水掻表ヨリ見ルノ圖

裏ニカ・フクリ有

コ・ニカ・フクリ有

同ク横ヨリ見ル圖

カ・フクリ
コ・ナリ

drop bombs. The technology for this certainly existed, but the extension of it to 'human gliders' or even 'human cannonballs' belongs to the realms of ninja fantasy.

CONDITIONS OF SERVICE

The ninja homelands

Two places are indelibly associated in the popular mind with ninja and ninjutsu. These are the Iga Province and the southern area of Omi Province known as Koga, and the bulk of historical evidence suggests that the popular view of Iga and Koga as the most important cradles of ninja is broadly correct. In the chronicle *Go kagami furoku* we read: 'There was a retainer of the family of Kawai Aki-no-kami of Iga, of pre-eminent skill in shinobi, and consequently for generations the name of people from Iga became established. Another tradition grew in Koga.'

In other words, the inhabitants of the Iga/Koga area (they share a common border) developed a certain expertise in the skills and techniques that were to become known as ninjutsu, and, more importantly, they hired themselves out as mercenaries until their province was sacked by Oda Nobunaga in 1581.

A brief glance at a map of medieval Japan gives one a clue as to why the Iga/Koga area could have the potential to produce a number of independent-minded families who by their military skills were sufficiently secure to be able to place these talents at the disposal of others. Iga Province (now the north-western part of Mie Prefecture) was entirely landlocked, and almost the whole length of its borders followed the tops of several ranges of mountains. Thus the villages in the flatlands within

Models of ninja equipment, most of which are described in this book, on show in the Ninja Museum at Iga Ueno.

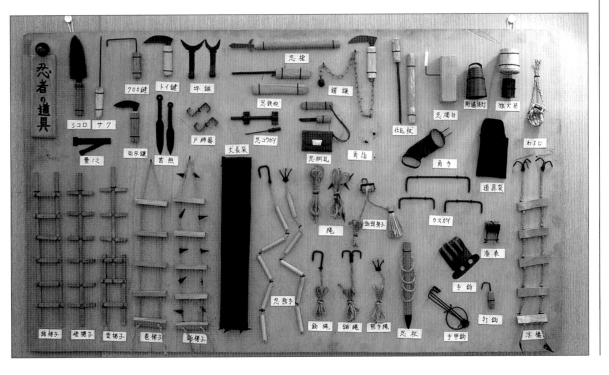

nestled inside a ring of natural defences, pierced only by steep mountain passes. The one side of Iga that is not entirely protected by mountains is the north, where it borders Koga, the southern portion of Omi Province. It was a situation somewhat analogous to that of contemporary Switzerland, though on a much smaller scale, where mountains provided such a good natural defence that its equally formidable inhabitants could become the mercenary soldiers of Europe.

A more detailed look at the topography also reveals that this was politically a very sensitive region. It lies just to the south of the 'neck' of medieval Japan, the narrow strip of land between Lake Biwa and the Bay of Owari that divides the country neatly in two. At the mouth of Lake Biwa lay the then capital, Kyoto, and from it ran the two main highways to the east: the Tokaido and the Nakasendo. The two roads were in fact one and the same as far as Kusatsu. The Tokaido then headed for the sea on the coast of Ise Province, just skirting north of Iga/Koga by the Suzuka Pass, then followed the Pacific coast. The Nakasendo turned north-east along the edge of Lake Biwa and threaded through the vast mountains of the 'Japan Alps' to join the Tokaido in the vicinity of modern Tokyo.

The Iga/Koga area thus formed a bridge between the main trade routes from the capital and the vast and wild mountains of the Kii Peninsula to the south. These mountains amaze one even today by the solitude they present for a region so close to the urban sprawl of Osaka and Kyoto. Within these mountains were villagers who lived their entire lives in one tiny valley community shut off from the rest of Japan until comparatively recent times, and visited only by the wandering yamabushi who traversed this wild country on their pilgrimages. Several accounts refer to these mountains as the haunt of bandits who acted as highwaymen along the Tokaido or as pirates on the sea coast of nearby Ise Province. Many of the ninja myths, such as that of the legendary outlaw Ishikawa Goemon who was supposed to be adept in ninjutsu, no doubt have their origin in the elaboration of the exploits of very un-magical gangs of robbers. The historian Sasama sums up the Iga situation as follows:

> In Iga Province at about the time of Onin, Jinki Iga-no-kami was provincial shugo, but thereafter for generations they declined and in Iga there were few who lived there to rule the ji-samurai (country samurai). The ji-samurai … were affiliated to families on the mountains and beaches of neighbouring provinces and were brigands and pirates, and lived by hunting and fishing. In later years the so-called Iga-shu began to be recruited to various provinces such as Odawara in groups of 50 men or 30 men and were used for ambushes.

The archaeological evidence presented by the numerous fortifications of Koga is also very revealing. Of 21 hilltop castle sites identified,

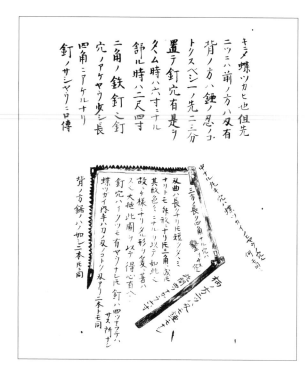

This clever folding saw, the ninja equivalent of a Swiss army knife, appears in *Bansen Shukai*.

many date from early in the Sengoku Period, evidence of tremendous military activity at the time. The various families were joined in a complex hierarchy of mutual support, thereby providing the ideal conditions for mercenary activity to flourish. The Wada family, for example, controlled a series of mountain-top fortresses along a river valley, and Wada Koremasa (1536–83) was sufficiently strong in Koga to give refuge there to the future shogun Ashikaga Yoshiaki after the suicide of his brother Ashikaga Yoshiteru in 1565.

Daily life in the ninja village

Like almost everything else in Japanese society the social structure within the ninja community of Iga Province was based on a rigid hierarchy. At the top of the tree were the *shonin*, who were the distinguished heads of families. Depending on his wealth, a shonin resembled either a minor daimyo or a village headman. Examples of shonin are the famous Hattori Hanzo, Momochi Sandayu and Fujibayashi Nagato-no-kami. Below the shonin were the *chujin*, who acted as the family's executive officers and leaders. The chunin would make arrangements for the hiring of ninja on a mercenary basis. Below them were the lowly *genin*, the ninja actually sent into action against an enemy.

The typical ninja village would be very different from a daimyo's bustling castle town, and at first sight would be virtually indistinguishable from any prosperous agricultural centre in a typical daimyo's territory. The big difference would be in the means employed for the village's defence, but these would be very subtle. So on the hills around there would be a chain of smoke beacons to give advance notice of any attack. Within the village itself the houses of the genin would be found on the outskirts, while the home of the shonin would be the village's central focus. This might consist of nothing more than a wooden farmhouse, but it would be located within a maze of rice fields which acted as a moat when flooded, as they would be for much of the year. Steep earthen banks and a bamboo fence or prickly hedge provided other defences. The paths between the rice fields were narrow, and a bell tower housed the means of alerting the villagers when danger threatened.

The ninja house

In several places in Japan today it is possible to visit so-called ninja houses that have been moved from their original locations and re-erected as tourist attractions. They inevitably contain various trap doors and hiding places, but how authentic are they?

It seems reasonable to conclude that a powerful and well-patronised shonin should turn his own techniques to his own advantage, and make his home as secure as possible against the surprise attacks that he

A ninja rocket, matching exactly contemporary Chinese descriptions, appears in this illustration from *Bansen Shukai*.

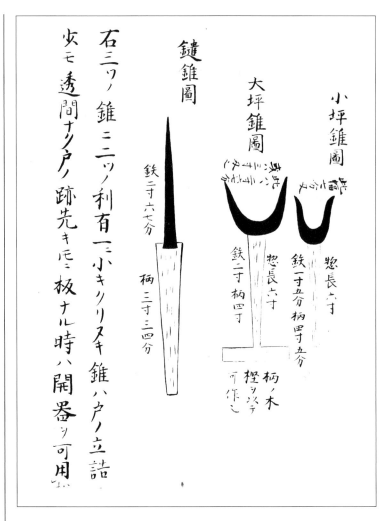

A selection of ninja 'burglars' tools from *Bansen Shukai*. See Plate B for full descriptions.

himself performed so well. As will be discussed below, the genuine fear of assassination made many powerful daimyo introduce well-authenticated features into their own mansions or castles. The most straightforward were features of building design that allowed a visitor to be monitored in secret by the shonin's guards, who could overpower an assassin in seconds. A loose floorboard, situated just to the side of where the shonin's arm would be when he held an audience, could conceal a sword ready for use. Sliding panels, so common in Japanese houses, could be redesigned to pivot around a central axis, so that a man could virtually disappear in the blinking of an eye. Staircases could be made to fold away, confusing any attacker. A trap door in a dark corridor could drop an assailant on to a row of poisoned spikes. A disappearing staircase that could be instantly retracted by standing on the protruding end after climbing it would also fool any pursuing ninja.

The most interesting example of a ninja-proofed house to have survived, and undoubtedly the most authentic, is the well-known Nijo jinya in Kyoto. This house situated quite near to Nijo castle was the house of Ogawa Nagatsuka, a former samurai who had become a rice merchant, and many of the so-called anti-ninja devices were in fact very sensible fire precautions, which is why it has survived for so long. Nevertheless, there are also several crime prevention features that were designed specifically to protect the owner from entry by unauthorised persons. These will be described in the later section on assassination.

NINJA CAMPAIGN LIFE

For the ninja, 'campaign life' had a totally different meaning from that of the conventional samurai or *ashigaru* (foot soldier). Ninja could be hired for specific, short-term operations or might be taken along with an army for campaigns of an unspecified or unknown duration. A siege, for example, could take months, during which ninja would be used for intelligence gathering or to cause confusion inside the castle.

Spying and espionage

The *Buke Meimokusho* illustrates the use of ninja for intelligence gathering and spying prior to a military campaign:

> Shinobi-monomi were people used in secret ways, and their duties were to go into the mountains and disguise themselves as firewood gatherers to discover and acquire the news about an enemy's territory … they were particularly expert at travelling in disguise.

These were the occasions when the disguise of a komuso would be most useful. The earliest written reference to ninja from Iga or Koga in action in this way occurs in the supplement to the *Nochi Kagami*, the annals of the Ashikaga shogunate. In one particular section we read: 'Concerning ninja, they were said to be from Iga and Koga, and went freely into enemy castles in secret. They observed hidden things, and were taken as being friends.'

The section goes on to mention a specific campaign in which Iga men were involved:

> Inside the camp at Magari of the Shogun Yoshihisa there were shinobi whose names were famous throughout the land. When Yoshihisa attacked Rokkaku Takayori, the family of Kawai Aki-no-kami of Iga, who served him at Magari earned considerable merit as shinobi in front of the great army of the Shogun. Since then successive generations of Iga men have been admired. This is the origin of the fame of the men of Iga.

The reference to the names of Rokkaku Takayori and the shogun Ashikaga Yoshihisa enables us to identify this action as one fought in the year 1487. Yoshihisa, who had been raised to the position of shogun at the age of nine by his father Yoshimasa, took steps to restore his family's military prowess as soon as he was of an age to do so. His chance came in 1487, when some 46 of the landowners of Omi Province, including a number from Koga, appealed to the shogun against the excesses of the shugo of Omi, Rokkaku Takayori, who was in the process of seizing everyone else's lands for himself. This in itself was nothing remarkable. The shugo were the provincial governors appointed by the Ashikaga, and the disorder of the Onin War had enabled many a shugo to disregard his obligation to the shogun and treat the territory entrusted to him as his own. But a proud young shogun, the most warlike of his family for a century, did not see such presumption as inevitable, and would not tolerate it. He therefore took personal charge of an expedition against Rokkaku Takayori and besieged him in his castle of Kannonji in Omi Province.

Young Yoshihisa set up camp at the nearby village of Magari. He was joined by several allies sympathetic to the cause of the shogunate and

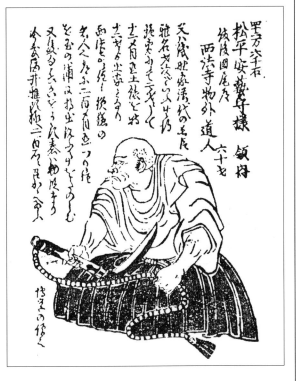

The *kusari gama*, the popular sickle and chain combination, shown here in an old martial-arts book illustration. The idea was to swing the weighted chain until it caught the opponent either by the sword arm or the leg, and finish him off with the sickle.

made good progress, but unfortunately Yoshihisa's physical health was not the equal of his mental condition. He was taken ill in camp and succumbed to a sickness from which he was eventually to die. His army therefore struck camp and returned to Kyoto. So by about 1487 the use as mercenaries of shinobi from Iga was well established. Unfortunately we do not know exactly how the ninja were used against Kannonji castle, but intelligence gathering was probably deployed.

The misty and mysterious Iga mountains, heartlands of the ninja. Iga was one of the most easily defensible provinces in Japan, and developed a tradition of very independent-minded leaders. It took the full force of the mighty Oda Nobunaga to conquer it.

Arson

Moving on 60 years from the *Nochi Kagami* account, there is good evidence of the use of ninja from Iga to set fire to buildings. The story is found in a reliable chronicle called the *Tamon-In nikki*, a diary kept by the Abbot Eishun of Tamon-In, a priory of the great Kofuku-ji monastery of Nara. The entry for the 26th day of the 11th month of the 10th Year of Tembun (1541) reads as follows:

> This morning, the sixth day of the 11th month of Tembun 10, the Iga shū entered Kasagi castle in secret and set fire to a few of the priests' quarters. They also set fire to outbuildings in various places inside the San no maru. They captured the Ichi no maru and the Ni no maru.

The word *maru* refers to the successive baileys of the castle. The chronicle goes on to identify the defender of Kasagi castle as a certain Kizawa Nagamasa, which allows us to sketch in some more details about the circumstances surrounding the action. In 1540 Kizawa Nagamasa's territory was invaded by the ambitious 17-year-old Miyoshi Chokei. The Kizawa army took up a position at Kasagi, where they were attacked by Miyoshi's ally, Tsutsui Junsho, so it is presumably Tsutsui Junsho who used the Iga ninja against the defenders. The men of Iga were worthy of their hire, for in the assault that followed the arson attack Kizawa Nagamasa was mortally wounded and the castle soon fell.

It is also interesting to note the presence inside Kasagi castle of a very famous family from the locality – the Yagyu. They were represented in the person of Yagyu Ieyoshi, father of Muneyoshi, who was later to found one of the most celebrated schools of swordsmanship in Japan. Yagyu village lay at the foot of Mount Kasagi, and when Kasagi fell the Yagyu continued the struggle, young Muneyoshi fighting the first battle of his life against the Tsutsui in 1544. A century later Muneyoshi's grandson, Jubei Mitsuyoshi, was to have tales told about his exploits as a ninja, so it is fascinating to see the family on the receiving end of ninjutsu in 1541.

These men from Iga clearly owed no vassal allegiance to any of the daimyo they served on campaign. Their service must therefore have been that of paid mercenaries, which is supported by the use of such words as 'hired', 'employed' and so on, although the nature of the payment remains a mystery. The whole topic of money was, however, regarded by samurai in general as unspeakably vulgar, so this is perhaps not so surprising.

Assassination

The best known of all ninja campaign activities, and the one most exaggerated by fiction and romance, was the ninja's role as the silent and deadly assassin. This is the image of the ninja *par excellence*, dressed in black, sneaking into the castle at the dead of night, and then polishing off his sleeping victim with knife or poison. During the Sengoku Period assassination by silent, expert, professional killers was often the only chance that rivals had of extinguishing the great daimyo who were customarily surrounded by bodyguards. Even though the fear of ninja assassination may have been exaggerated out of all proportion to the actual risk, there was no sense in taking any chances.

The measures taken to protect against assassinations can be seen in various locations in Japan to this day. Castles were of course very well defended. The private quarters at Inuyama castle, for example, have wooden sliding doors at the rear, behind which armed guards would always be at the ready. The design of the approach to a castle could be arranged so that a visitor was under observation from the moment he entered the outermost gate. Blind spots and dark shadowy areas could also be 'designed out', and the ultimate example must be Himeji castle, where the approach to the keep is made via a labyrinth of passages and paths.

In fact an entire building could theoretically be 'ninja-proofed', as shown by the famous and extraordinary 'nightingale floor' built in Nijo castle in Kyoto. As thousands of tourists discover every year, it is

A ninja assassin drops from the ceiling of the Ninja Museum in Iga Ueno.

The ninja girl attendant at the Ninja house in Iga Ueno demonstrates how a rotating door works.

impossible to walk along the highly polished corridors without raising the tuneful squeaking from the carefully counterbalanced floorboards that was likened to the sound of a nightingale singing and gave warning of an approaching assassin. The clothes that were required to be worn at the shogun's court also helped the Tokugawa family. The long *naga-bakama*, the wide trousers that actually covered the feet and had to be dragged behind as one walked, made an assassination attempt on the shogun almost a physical impossibility.

Outside his castle or his mansion, a daimyo would be at his most vulnerable when recovering from wounds, for which purpose a number of 'secret springs' would be maintained. The Japanese have appreciated from very early days the healing power of natural springs. Japan is thus dotted with hot-spring resorts, and a daimyo would have had his own in distant locations deep in the mountains which ninja could not find.

The confusion of the battlefield might also allow the opportunity for an assassination to take place. The daimyo's battlefield headquarters consisted of an area screened off by a curtain called a *maku*, and he would be heavily guarded. The most loyal samurai would form an impenetrable ring round their lord if danger threatened. Nevertheless several examples exist of assassination attempts being made.

In spite of all precautions there were few daimyo who were not subject to some form of assassination attempt. They therefore lived their lives surrounded by loyal bodyguards who kept their lord under constant protection, never separated from him by more than a thin wood and paper screen. Matsuura Shigenobu, the daimyo of Hirado island, kept a heavy club in his bathroom. Mori Motonari reckoned that a daimyo should trust no one, particularly relatives – a wise precept illustrated by the case of Saito Toshimasa, who had made an early career change from Buddhist priest to oil merchant and became a daimyo in his own right by murdering his adoptive father. Hojo Soun acquired his future base of Odawara castle by arranging for the young owner to be murdered while out hunting. Even the powerful Oda Nobunaga was eventually to meet his end from a night attack on his sleeping quarters by a rival, though it took a small army rather than one ninja to do it.

Takeda Shingen, who apparently had two doors on his lavatory, is recorded as recommending that even when alone with his wife a daimyo should keep his dagger close at hand. One unsuccessful attempt on his life was made by a ninja called Hachisuka Tenzo, sent by Oda Nobunaga. Tenzo was forced to flee, and the Takeda samurai pursued him into a wood, where he concealed himself from the moonlight among the shadows of the trees. A spear thrust from his pursuers caught only his costume, and he subsequently evaded capture by hiding in a hole in the ground, which he had already prepared. Nobunaga's chosen assassin may

Another rotating door, this time at the other ninja house in Koga. It looks like an ordinary sliding door found in any Japanese house.

well have been an Iga man, for we know that he had some on his payroll.

Oda Nobunaga's ruthless ways of waging war made him the target of several assassination attempts. Rokkaku Yoshisuke, who had seen his territory in Omi Province invaded by Nobunaga in 1571, hired a Koga ninja called Sugitani Zenjubo, whose particular speciality was sharpshooting with the long-barrelled arquebus. Zenjubo lay in wait for Nobunaga as he was crossing the Chigusa Pass between Omi and Mino Provinces, and fired twice, presumably with two separate guns. Both bullets struck home, but were absorbed by Nobunaga's armour and the padded shoulder protectors beneath. Zenjubo escaped to the mountains, but was apprehended four years later and tortured to death.

The year 1573 witnessed an attempt on Nobunaga's life by a certain Manabe Rokuro, the chief steward of a vassal of the daimyo Hatano Hideharu. Oda Nobunaga destroyed the Hatano in 1573, and Manabe Rokuro was instructed to take revenge. He tried to sneak into Nobunaga's castle of Azuchi and to stab Nobunaga while he was asleep in his bedroom, but was discovered and captured by two of the guards. He then committed suicide, and his body was displayed in the local market place to discourage any other would-be killers.

The semi-legendary ninja Ishikawa Goemon is credited with another attempt on Nobunaga's life. He hid in the ceiling above the victim's bedroom and tried to drip poison down a thread into Nobunaga's mouth. But the most remarkable assassination attempt on Nobunaga is recorded in the *Iranki*. Three ninja each took aim at Nobunaga with large-calibre firearms when he was inspecting the ruinous state of Iga

The ninja girl attendant at the Ninja house in Iga Ueno demonstrates how a low trapdoor can give access to the garden.

Province that his invasion had brought about. The shots missed their target, but killed seven of Nobunaga's companions.

Other examples of assassinations that failed include Tokugawa Ieyasu's sending of a ninja called Kirigakure Saizo to murder his rival Toyotomi Hideyoshi. Saizo hid beneath the floor of Hideyoshi's dwelling, but a guard managed to pin him through the arm with the blade of his spear, which he had thrust at random through the floorboards. Another ninja, presumably in the service of Hideyoshi, then 'smoked him out' using a primitive flamethrower.

Who killed Kenshin?

The most famous ninja assassination story is of how Uesugi Kenshin was murdered in his lavatory by a ninja who had concealed himself in the sewage pit, and who thrust a spear or sword up Kenshin's anus at the crucial moment. Kenshin died a few days later, and it was suspected that Oda Nobunaga had sent the assassin. The succeeding months only served to emphasise the benefits to Nobunaga, because Kenshin's nephew and adopted heir fought each other for the inheritance, thus weakening the Uesugi immeasurably.

The actual circumstances surrounding Kenshin's death are quite well recorded, and do not necessarily contradict the ninja theory, because he appears to have suffered some form of crisis, probably a stroke, while in his lavatory. The *Kenshin Gunki* states that, 'on the 9th day of the 3rd month he had a stomach ache in his toilet. This unfortunately persisted until the 13th day when he died.'

The strongest evidence against death from anything other than natural causes comes from accounts of the months leading up to Kenshin's death, when he composed a poem concerned with his apprehension that his life was coming to an end. In other words, in the days leading up to the catastrophe in his toilet he was already anticipating death, and it was no surprise to him when it came. Kenshin was also a very heavy drinker, and sometime during the ninth month of 1577 held state with several of his closest retainers, to whom Naoe Kanetsugu later confided his fears for their daimyo's condition. Naoe observed that Kenshin had seemed to get sicker as every day went by. So what was wrong with him? An important clue is given in another diary that noted that in the middle of that winter Uesugi Kenshin was getting very thin, with a pain in his chest 'like an iron ball'. He often vomited his food, and soon was forced to take only cold water. All the symptoms point to cancer of the stomach or oesophagus, with the 'iron ball' being the actual tumour. Stomach cancer is still a very common cause of death in Japan, and is also associated with heavy drinking. The knowledge of his illness would of course have been kept a closely guarded secret lest Nobunaga found out, so if a ninja had been despatched it would have

A narrow ladder with trap door beneath in the ninja house at Koga.

Ninja in traditional costume with essential personal equipment

A

Ninja specialised equipment and its use

Ninja development, training and recruitment

C

A ninja disguised as a yamabushi returns home to his village in Iga province

D

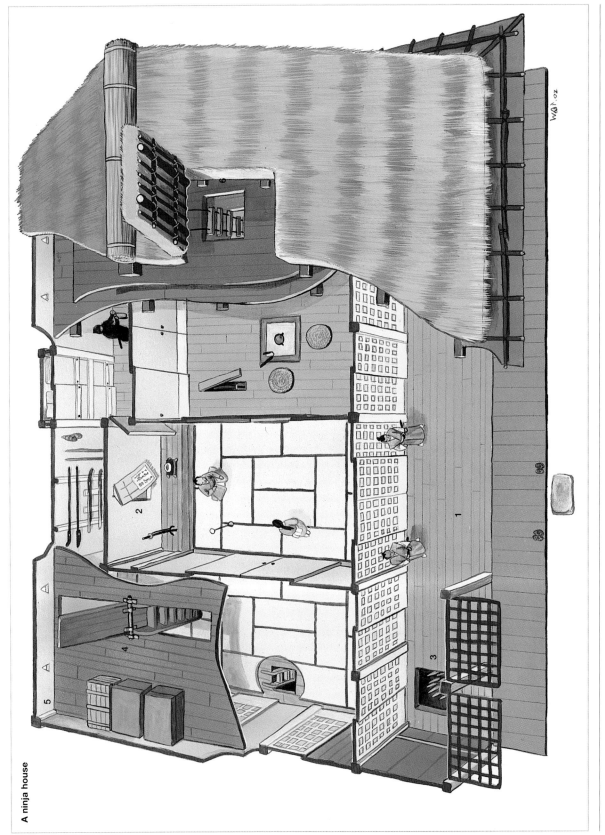

A ninja house

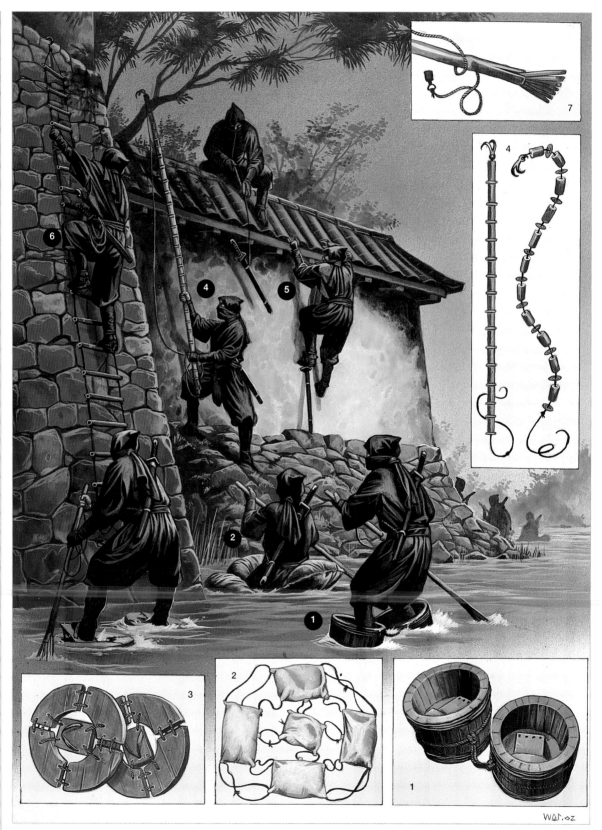

F Ninja on campaign 1: Entering a castle

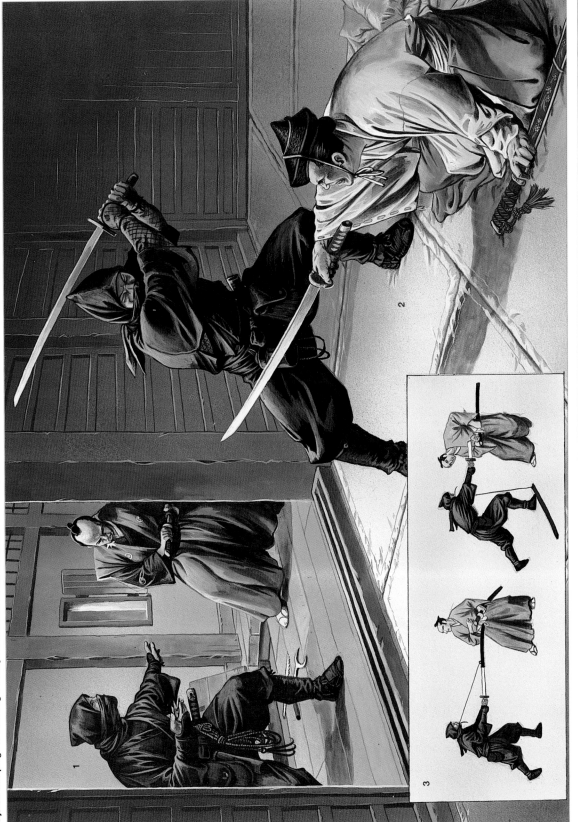

Ninja in battle: A castle raid during a siege

been without the knowledge that his victim had only months or perhaps weeks to live. Kenshin's close retainers knew of the tumour in his stomach, so a sudden crisis may have been recognised by them as a distinct possibility. If this were so, then Nobunaga's ninja may well have unwittingly committed the perfect crime.

An assassination attempt

Reference was made earlier to the house in Kyoto called Nijo jinya that exhibits several protective measures against ninja assassinations. Let us examine these using a hypothetical attempt on the life of its owner, Ogawa Nagatsuka.

The group of three ninja sent to kill him are operating as a team, and even if only one of their number survives to land the final blow, their task will have been accomplished. Ogawa is presently sitting in the o-zashiki, the main hall of the house, and is having a conversation with a trusted ninja whom Ogawa sent to spy on a rival disguised as a yamabushi. He arrived as expected at the front porch, where he removed his footwear and was escorted along the corridor by a guard. In keeping with tradition, he placed his sword in a rack at the entrance to the o-zashiki. Ogawa, however, suspects that the man might be a double agent, and this is confirmed when he suddenly kicks aside the low table dividing them and lunges at Ogawa with a concealed dagger. Ogawa is ready. He was apparently cooling himself with an ordinary fan, but the fan has iron staves and these are sufficient to parry the blow just long enough for the assassin to be tackled from an unexpected direction. From where the ninja is sitting the skylight in the ceiling above them looks just like a window, but he does not know that it hides a secret room where Ogawa's bodyguard has been watching every move and listening to every sound. Almost as the assassin moves the guard drops on to his back.

This gives Ogawa the opportunity to retrieve the sword hidden in a secret compartment at his side. His bodyguard has dealt with the assassin, who now lies dead before him, but Ogawa knows that there are probably others lurking. He pulls back the sliding door and enters the narrow hallway. He can hear the squeaking of the nightingale floor as someone runs from the front door. Whoever it is has not called out to him, so it probably isn't one of his own men. Ogawa takes no chances, and where the corridor turns there is an apparent blind corner. But the artistic-looking timbers provide a staircase to a concealed room above, entered by an innocuous-looking opening. Ogawa scrambles in. He is not a moment too soon, because two ninja come flying down the hallway. They run straight past his hiding place and come to the end of the corridor where the entrance to Ogawa's bathroom is. On the wall beside it is a shelf. They do not know that it is in fact a hidden staircase that could be dropped down and as easily pulled up again. Ogawa could have used it had he not employed the other device earlier.

The upstairs window of Nijo jinya in Kyoto. The glazing is a modern addition.

The guard has now arrived behind the two ninja. One goes into the bathroom to search for Ogawa. The other turns and slashes at the guard, but his sword catches on a low beam. This allows the guard to leap into the small tea room as a shuriken whizzes over his shoulder. He jumps into a closet, which the ninja slashes at furiously with his sword, only to reveal a back door through which the guard has slipped into an adjacent room and then out into the garden. In the garden are hiding places for valuables. The ornamental rocks could also be used as weapons, but for now it will be the scene of a sword fight to the death.

Meanwhile the other ninja, having found no signs of Ogawa on the ground floor, has run back along the corridor and up the fixed staircase to the first floor. However, as a precaution some time before the guest arrived, Ogawa's guard removed two floor panels as ankle breakers. In the dark the ninja stumbles into the first of these holes and is momentarily off guard. Ogawa's man lunges at him, and even though it only produces a slight flesh wound the ninja is knocked down the cul-de-sac stairway into the room below.

However, his companion has killed the other guard in the garden and on returning to the hallway has guessed the real nature of the shelf. He swings his sword at it and when it falls he runs upstairs. This has taken him into a room immediately adjacent to the one in which Ogawa was concealed, but Ogawa has already left his first hiding place and climbed up into the top storey of the building via a retractable rope ladder. In the dark it looks as though it is a solid ceiling. The ninja hears a noise from along the corridor and runs along to where his companion has disappeared down the stairs. He realises that his comrade is dead when two guards come running up the stairs towards him. Running back into the room above which Ogawa is now concealed, the ninja swings his sword at the lattice window and breaks it to pieces. He crashes through and lands in the courtyard outside. He has no companions now to help him scale the wall, so he rips out the suspensory cord from his sword as he leans it against the wall and jumps up using the sword-guard as a step. The last the Ogawa guards see of the ninja is his sword winging its way over the wall behind him. Their master is safe and two ninja are dead. It was a successful night's work for them.

Nijo jinya's courtyard and entrance. Unfortunately no photography is permitted inside this fascinating building.

NINJA IN WAR

For a ninja, the distinction between peacetime and wartime operations was blurred, but when a daimyo was engaged in a major military campaign a ninja's role could be greatly enhanced. Ninja could be employed for intelligence gathering prior to an attack, or used on a battlefield to cause confusion in the enemy ranks. Ninja were also very useful in longer-term siege warfare, either as spies, arsonists or assassins or in other roles. All the examples that follow are taken from authentic and reliable historical accounts.

Ninja at Sawayama, 1558

The first example concerns the Rokkaku family of Omi Province. A member of the Rokkaku family, Rokkaku Takayori, was mentioned earlier for having had ninja used against him by the shogun Yoshihisa in 1487. In 1558 or thereabouts his grandson, Rokkaku Yoshikata, fought a campaign against a treacherous retainer called Dodo, who fortified himself within Sawayama castle, the site of which is near the present town of Hikone. In spite of a siege that lasted many days Yoshikata could not budge him, and he decided to employ a ninja from Iga called Tateoka Doshun.

Doshun must have been of chunin rank, because we read of him leading into action in person his team of 48 ninja, of whom 44 were from Iga and four from Koga. He proposed using a ninja technique called *bakemono-jutsu* (ghost technique) which was a very dramatic title for an absurdly simple operation. Doshun stole one of the paper lanterns that bore Dodo's family *mon* (badge). Several replicas were constructed, and Doshun and his men calmly walked straight in through the front gate! Once safely inside they started to set fire to the castle, and so secret were their activities that Dodo's garrison concluded that traitors had emerged from within their own midst. In spite of heroic efforts to extinguish the fire, panic began to spread as quickly as the flames. At this point Rokkaku Yoshikata ordered his main army into a victorious final assault.

Yagyu Muneyoshi, who is popularly supposed to have been a ninja, as depicted on his statue at Yagyu. (Nara Prefecture)

Ninja at Maibara, 1561

The next example from 1561 illustrates the mercenary nature of the ninja very well: first, because they refuse to move into action other than on their own terms, and second, because we see a certain Kizawa Nagamasa using Iga ninja against the same Rokkaku Yoshikata who had employed them in 1558! In 1561 Kizawa Nagamasa tried to re-take the castle of Maibara (then called Futo) to the east of Lake Biwa, which had recently fallen to the Rokkaku. Nagamasa placed matters in the capable hands of two commanders called Imai Kenroku and Isono Tamba-no-kami. They in turn engaged the assistance of three genin from Iga to mount a night attack as a prelude to a more conventional assault. In the *Shima kiroku* we read that, 'the Iga shu entered in secret, started fires in the castle, and at this signal the keep and second bailey were conquered,' and in the *Asai Sandaiki* we read that, 'We employed shinobi-no-mono of Iga. … They were contracted to set fire to the castle.'

Such are the bare bones of the action, but things did not go quite according to plan. On the night of the 1st day of the 7th month the Iga

Prince Yamato, whose skills at assassination make him the spiritual ancestor of Japan's ninja.

An assassination is carried out through a sliding door.

ninja were in position and the 'conventional' forces had begun to move forward. But it soon became clear to Imai Kenroku, stationed on a nearby hill, that the ninja had not moved into action. When he complained about their hesitation he received the reply that a samurai from north of Lake Biwa could not possibly understand ninja tactics, and that he would have to wait for a propitious moment. But by now the 'conventional' army was on the move. The fire attack was late, and the ninja, in the manner of mercenaries the world over, implied by their refusal to attack until ready that unless allowed to conduct warfare in their own way they would all go home. The ninja leader suggested that Imai Kenroku should regroup his forces. If he withdrew for about an hour, the ninja would raid the castle, and the signal to move forward would be fire appearing from it.

This Imai Kenroku agreed to do, but the results were almost disastrous. His army blundered across the front of his comrade Isono Tamba-no-kami, who appears not to have been informed about the manoeuvre, and the samurai of the latter army drew the conclusion that a dawn attack had been made on them from the castle. A horseman in the front line called Kishizawa Yoichi sprang into action in an attempt to be first into the battle. He also observed, just ahead of him, the 'enemy' commander, so he galloped forward, and the unfortunate Imai Kenroku, trying desperately to control the night march of his army, received Yoichi's spear thrust in his back. Being totally unprepared for any assault, as he knew there were only friendly troops behind him, Imai was too shocked to give any resistance and fell dead from his horse. The two armies began fighting each other, and 20 were killed before order was restored. By then the ninja had set fire to the castle, and the two shattered allies joined forces to attack it. Futo eventually fell, to everyone's relief, but at quite a price.

Ninja at Udono, 1562

The example that follows shows ninja in a much better light. The complicated background is as follows. When ImagawaYoshimoto was killed at the battle of Okehazama in 1560 his followers rushed to abandon the cause of his doomed family and join the victorious Oda Nobunaga. The future shogun Tokugawa Ieyasu wanted to change sides, but the late Imagawa Yoshimoto had a son, Ujizane, who held a number of hostages from Ieyasu's own family, including his wife and son, whose throats would surely be cut at the least indication of a change of allegiance. Ieyasu's problem was solved by one dramatic stroke in the year 1562.

The Imagawa's western outpost was a castle called Kaminojo, held for them by a certain Udono Nagamochi. It promised to be a useful prize for the Oda, and if Ieyasu was able to capture it quickly on Nobunaga's behalf any hostages taken from Kaminojo could be exchanged for Ieyasu's own family. It would of course have to be done quickly before the news got out and Imagawa had a chance to murder them. The source for the action, the *Mikawa Go Fudoki*, takes the story on:

Mitsuhara Sanza'emon said, 'As this castle is built upon a formidable precipice we will be condemning many of our allies to suffer great losses. But by good fortune there are among the go-hatamoto some men associated with the Koga-shu of Omi Province. Summon the Koga-shu through their compatriots and then they can sneak into the castle.'

The leader of the men of Koga was a certain Tomo Sukesada. He engaged over 80 ninja and:

This group were ordered to lie down and hide in several places, and on the night of the fifteenth day of the third month sneaked inside the castle. Before long they were setting fire to towers inside the fortress.

In other words, they carried out a classic ninja raid under cover of darkness. The *Mikawa Go Fudo ki* account, however, adds some interesting points of detail. First, the raiding party deliberately made as little sound as possible while they ran around killing, so that the defenders thought they were traitors from within the garrison. The ninja

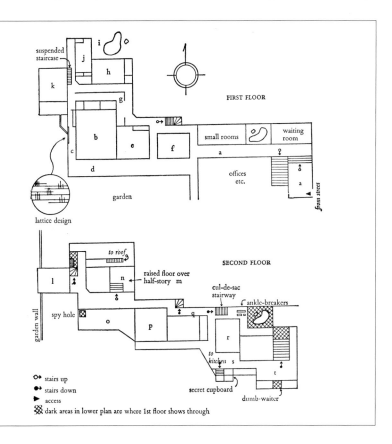

Plan of Nijo jinya in Kyoto. The plan is keyed as follows to enable the reader to follow the hypothetical assassination attempt described in the text. (a) the street entrance (see photograph on p.42); (b) o-zashiki, the 15-mat reception room; (c) and (d) the corridor; (e) 8-mat room; (f) 6-mat room; (g) hallway giving access to the concealed half-storey above; (h) 6-mat room looking out on the garden; (i) garden, with places for hiding valuables; (j) small tea room, its closet has a secret door; (k) the daimyo's bath house: outside in the corridor is a stairway that looks like a shelf but can be lowered; (l) upstairs room allowing emergency escape (see photograph of windows viewed from outside on p.41); (m) concealed room; (n) tea room on raised floor over concealed room; (o) concealed guard room above reception room; (p) 8-mat room; (q) narrow landing with low ceiling to limit swordplay and ankle-breaking exposed beams; (r) small tea room; (s) dark hallway with modern staircase at front; (t) modern hallway. (Plan reproduced from Kyoto: *A Contemplative Guide* by G Mosher, by kind permission of Tuttle and Co.)

45

were also dressed like the defenders, thereby causing confusion, and as they spread out they communicated with one another using a password:

> … the garrison were utterly defeated and fled. The keeper of the castle, Nagamochi, fled to beside the Hall of Prayers on the north side of the castle, where Tomo Sukesada discovered his whereabouts, came running up, thrust his spear at him, and took his head as he lay prostrate. His sons Fujitaro Nagateru and Katsusaburo Nagatada were captured alive by Tomo Suketsuna.

Two hundred of the Udono garrison were burned to death in the conflagration that followed, but this was of less importance to Ieyasu than the priceless reward of Udono's two sons as hostages. Following the battle Ieyasu sent a *kanshajo* (letter of commendation) to Tomo Sukesada praising the service he had rendered at Kaminojo. It is preserved in the archives of the Iwane, a prominent family of Koga:

> This is concerning the time when Udono Fujitaro Nagateru was defeated. Such renown has not been equalled in recent times. Since that time I have been occupied with one thing and another and have neglected to write for some years. (I wish you) good health, and have the honour to congratulate you. I have been pleased to listen to the particulars of the matter despatched by both my retainers Matsui Sakon Tadatsugu and Sakai Masachika.

A model of a ninja climbing a rope, from the Iga Ueno Ninja Museum.

As the only kanshajo in history addressed to a leader of ninja, the letter provides unique written proof of the value Ieyasu placed on their particular abilities. However, the affair of the two sons of Udono was not quite over. As part of the hostage agreement, Ieyasu allowed Imagawa Ujizane to keep what was left of Kaminojo castle, and after its repair Ujizane reappointed the Udono brothers as its defenders. Having already suffered one defeat at the hands of Ieyasu the pair began a rather unwise policy of outwardly supporting the raids into Mikawa Province by the Buddhist fanatics of the Ikko sect. The raids particularly infuriated a certain Matsudaira Kiyoyoshi, whose relatives had been held hostage but had not been part of the deal struck over the fall of Kaminojo. They had subsequently been put to death by impaling them on sharp stakes, so Kiyoyoshi took his revenge by launching a furious attack on Kaminojo castle:

> But, as might be expected, the Udono brothers defended it vigorously, and the attackers were thoroughly beaten, many being either wounded or killed in action. On hearing that the attacking force were on the

point of being defeated His Lordship set out in great haste, set up his army in camp on Natoriyama, and sent men of Koga who attacked the castle. Taking advantage of an unguarded point they made a commotion in the castle as Ieyasu had ordered them to. The Udono brothers had run out of defensive techniques. Fujitaro gathered seven samurai about him, but when they were all killed the castle fell.

That was the end of the Udono brothers, who had earned their place in history by being the only samurai to have been defeated by the same ninja twice.

Ninja at Sekigahara, 1600

When the second unifier of Japan, Toyotomi Hideyoshi, died in 1598 his son Toyotomi Hideyori was only five years old, and a coterie of jealous daimyo began to intrigue among themselves, all eager to be seen as the infant Hideyori's protector. Tokugawa Ieyasu played off one rival against another, until all the daimyo were divided into two armed camps. Matters were resolved in the autumn of 1600 with the cataclysmic battle of Sekigahara, the largest battle ever fought on Japanese soil. The ninja of Iga and Koga, who were now retainers of the Tokugawa, played their part in the campaign.

The preliminary moves of the battle of Sekigahara consisted of a spate of attacks and sieges on castles, including the castle of Fushimi to the south-east of Kyoto. It was held for Ieyasu's 'Eastern Army' by the Torii family, who held off the 'Western Army' for as long as they could manage, thus giving Ieyasu's forces time to move into position from the east. The Torii were helped in their defence by the actions of several hundred warriors from Koga, some of whom were inside the castle, while others harassed the besiegers from outside. About 100 were killed in the

Girl ninja from the Iga Ueno Ninja House pose for the camera.

fighting, and after the successful conclusion of the Sekigahara campaign Ieyasu held a memorial service for their spirits.

The actual battle of Sekigahara began at dawn on a foggy autumn morning, and was fought for the best part of the day on a restricted front between large mountains. There is only one account of undercover operations of any sort at Sekigahara, yet this one is unique and was in fact carried out by the Shimazu clan of Satsuma against the Tokugawa. The Shimazu appear to have developed an extraordinary gunnery tactic whereby sharpshooters were deliberately left behind when an army retreated to act, in effect, as 'human booby traps'.

Towards the end of the fighting the Satsuma samurai were forced to retreat before the fierce charge of the 'Red Devils' of Ii Naomasa, who dressed all his followers in brilliant red-lacquered armour. On came the Ii samurai to where a number of 'human booby traps' were lying in wait. One spotted Ii Naomasa coming towards him and fired a bullet which went through the horse's belly and shattered Naomasa's right elbow. Both man and horse collapsed, and Naomasa had to be carried from the field.

There is an interesting addition to the story, because the wounded Ii Naomasa received first-aid from a ninja in his own service, Miura Yo'emon, who was the joshin (chief vassal) of the Ii. He was an Iga man, and Ieyasu had presented him to Ii Naomasa in 1583. When Naomasa was shot Yo'emon gave him some black medicine to drink which was designed to help stop the bleeding. The Miura's residential quarter in Hikone is remembered today as Iga-machi.

Ninja at Osaka, 1615

The victory of Sekigahara was almost totally decisive. Tokugawa Ieyasu was proclaimed shogun in 1603, and reigned from Edo castle where his Iga and Koga men provided a secure guard. The Iga men's duties included guarding the innermost parts of the palace, which were known as the O-oku. Here were the quarters of the shogun's concubines. The Koga group, who were half the number of their Iga comrades, guarded the great outer gate of the castle called the Ote mon.

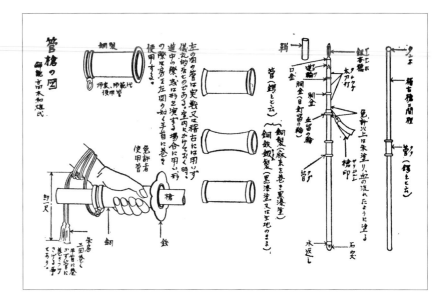

A collapsible and extendable spear, a weapon used more widely than by ninja alone. An assailant's victim would expect the spear to have only a short shaft, and would not back away far enough.

In 1614 the ninja were back in action again on the battlefield, when Toyotomo Hideyori, now grown to manhood, gathered into his late father's massive fortress of Osaka tens of thousands of disaffected samurai who had suffered from the Tokugawa seizure of power. The challenge was too great for Ieyasu to ignore, and in the winter of 1614 he laid siege to Osaka's walls, which measured almost 12 miles in perimeter. The Tokugawa side used ninja from both Iga and Koga under Hattori Masanari and Yamaoka Kagetsuge respectively. One of Ieyasu's leading commanders at the siege of Osaka was Ii Naotaka, who had inherited his father's territories and his red-clad samurai army, so it is not surprising to note the name of Miura Yo'emon in his service. Miura went to the Nabari area of Iga to recruit ninja for use in the siege; they fought in the army as well as carrying out individual operations.

The Osaka garrison had strengthened the outer defences by constructing a barbican out into the moat called the Sanada-maru. An attack was carried out on the 4th day of the 12th month, and was led by Ii Naotaka, who crossed the dry moat beneath the barbican's walls. Because there was a dense morning fog the attackers found it difficult to advance, and a hail of bullets came from within the castle. Casualties were mounting as the Ii's comrades galloped forwards and called for a retreat, but because of the noisy melee the order was scarcely heard.

A ninja jumping off a castle wall in a shot kindly arranged by the Iga Ueno City Department of Tourism. This is the classic image of the acrobatic ninja superman. **49**

Miura Yo'emon, who was currently removing arrowheads from the wounded, ordered his ninja into action in a move that showed a subtle understanding of the samurai mind. They approached the mass of men in the moat and fired on them at random. Their comrades, surprised by the arrows that came flying at them from behind, turned towards them and thus 'attacked to safety', the need for an actual 'retreat' having been avoided. On another occasion a ten-man ninja unit entered the castle with the aim of creating discord between the commanders. We know that one of the commanders did in fact commit suicide around this time, so ninja may have been involved.

This first half of the Osaka siege, known as the Winter Campaign of Osaka, came to an end with a spurious peace treaty that led to the flattening of the outer defence works. In the summer of 1615 Ieyasu returned to the fray and laid siege again to the now weakened castle. The ninja of the Winter Campaign had returned to Iga somewhat dissatisfied with their rewards, and had to be summoned once again by Miura – evidence that even at this late stage those not in the direct service of the Tokugawa were still behaving like mercenaries. Here they lent a form of service similar in vein to that of the winter operation when there was an incident at the headquarters of the general Okayama Kansuke. So many camp followers and local people had swarmed into Okayama's camp that observation of the enemy had become impossible, and military operations were severely restricted. Miura applied his ninja version of crowd control by firing randomly into the multitude, who quickly dispersed.

There were apparently two or three wounded persons in the unit of Todo Takatora, who was nonplussed and in fact praised the ninja for their action. It is not surprising that Todo understood ninja, for he had taken part in Nobunaga's Iga invasion of 1581, and had subsequently been granted part of Iga as his fief. Following Tokugawa Ieyasu's recommendation he fortified his territory by erecting the present-day Ueno castle on the site of the temple where the Iga warriors had assembled during the Iga Revolt.

The 'Summer Campaign' of Osaka was finally settled by a fierce pitched battle at Tennô-ji to the south of the castle. The Ii ninja unit fought alongside the regular troops, and as evidence of their success a record states:

Item, one head: Miura Yo'emon
In the same unit:
Item, two heads: Shimotani Sanzo
Item, one head: Okuda Kasa'emon
Item, one head: Saga Kita'emon.

As the defenders retreated back into the castle, Ii Naotaka opened up on the keep with a

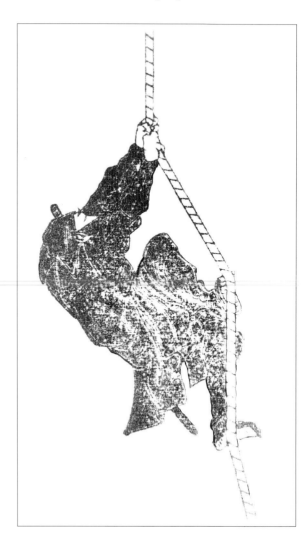

It is not generally known that Japan's great artist Hokusai included just one picture of a ninja in his voluminous *Manga* (sketchbooks). Here he is, climbing a rope in classic ninja style.

number of very heavy cannon and the castle fell. Toyotomi Hideyori committed suicide as Osaka blazed around him.

Ninja at Shimabara, 1638

The fall of Osaka castle meant the disappearance of the last major threat to the Tokugawa shogunate that was to arise for the next two and a half centuries. The one serious outbreak of armed strife that occurred during the Tokugawa rule happened in 1638 at Shimabara in Kyushu, where what began as a peasant farmers' protest developed into a full-scale revolt. The Shimabara Rebellion has always attracted the attention of Western historians because of the overtly Christian nature of much of its motivation. Christianity had been banned in Japan in 1637, after much sporadic persecution. No foreigner was allowed to land in Japan, and no Japanese was allowed to leave. Shimabara thus provided a focus for persecuted Christians as well as rebellious farmers, although the latter had grievance enough. The local daimyo, Matsukura Shigemasa, was an oppressive tyrant given to punishing those of the lower orders who offended him by dressing them in straw raincoats and setting fire to the straw.

An assassin of 'half ninja' form, observing his intended victims through the translucent shoji screen as he waits in the garden. It is illustrations like this that have given rise to today's popular image of the ninja.

Matters came to a head when the insurgents fortified themselves in the dilapidated old castle of Hara on the Shimabara peninsula and defied all local attempts to defeat them. Eventually the shogun, Tokugawa Iemitsu, mounted a full-scale expeditionary force from Edo, and the Tokugawa samurai were plunged into a world they thought had gone for ever. It is not surprising to see the ninja of Koga returned to their earlier roles of siege warfare, and the records of their activities, which are quite well detailed, contain some of the best accounts of ninja in action at any time. A good summary comes from a diary kept by a descendant of Ukai Kan'emon:

> 1st month 6th day
> They were ordered to reconnoitre the plan of construction of Hara castle, and surveyed the distance from the defensive moat to the ni no maru, the depth of the moat, the conditions of roads, the height of the wall, and the shape of the loopholes.

The results were put on a detailed plan by the guard Kanematsu Tadanao, and sent to Edo and presented for inspection by the shogun, Tokugawa Iemitsu. A further account of the fighting, the *Amakusa gunki*, the journal of Matsudaira Kai-no-kami Kagetsuna, tells us:

> 15th day. Men from Koga in Omi Province who concealed their appearance would steal up to the castle every night and go inside as they pleased.

The Ukai diary describes a particular raid by the Koga men to deprive the garrison of provisions:

1st month 21st day
The so-called Hara castle raid was a provisions raid, by the orders of the Commander-in-Chief Matsudaira Nobutsuna. They raided from the Kuroda camp near the western beach and cooperated in the capture of thirteen bags of provisions which the enemy depended on as a lifeline. This night also they infiltrated the enemy castle and obtained secret passwords.

In his account of the provisions raid in his book *The Nobility of Failure*, Ivan Morris mentions the ninja action, but adds the strange detail that they had ropes attached to their legs so that their dead bodies could be

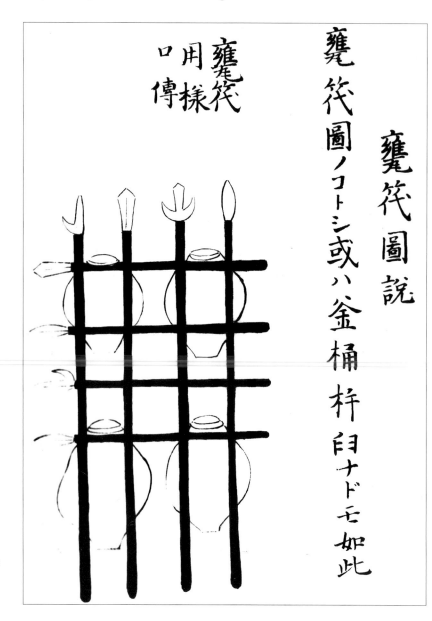

Spears and jars combined to produce a booby-trap over a hole in this picture from *Bansen Shukai*. The spears would be covered with grass.

pulled back. This seems such an unlikely course of action that I am assuming that Morris has mistranslated the idiomatic expression 'life-line' which appears in the account.

The most exciting raid happened six days later, and is recorded in the Ukai diary. The commander of the Tokugawa force, Matsudaira Nobutsuna, was unsure about the condition of the enemy garrison inside the castle. He suspected that provisions would be running low, so he despatched the ninja inside to gather information. The Koga men were advised that only two or three out of their number could expect to return alive. Volunteers were found in the persons of Mochizuki Yo'emon, Arakawa Shichirobei, Natsume Shika-no-suke, Yamanaka Judaiyu and Tomo Gohei, whose surname appears in a list of those involved in the attack on Kaminojo in 1562 – a nice illustration of the continuity of the ninja tradition:

1st month 27th day
We dispersed spies who were prepared to die inside Hara castle. Then we raided at midnight from the Hosokawa camp, and those who went on the reconnaissance in force captured an enemy flag; both Arakawa Shichirobei and Mochizuki Yo'emon met extreme resistance and suffered from their serious wounds for forty days.

A very noisy diversion was provided by the arquebus squad under Hosokawa, who fired a volley into the open sky, a technique known as 'the hundred cloud gun'. This had the additional intention, which succeeded admirably, of permitting the ninja to attack under cover of darkness, for no sooner had the guns erupted than the defenders immediately doused all the lights, which were customarily provided from pine torches round the perimeter and within the castle. The garrison sentries were of course on full alert, but the ninja concealed themselves in some brushwood and waited until the defenders relaxed their guard later in the night.

When it was quiet they scaled the walls using the ninja climbing equipment described earlier. Arakawa and Mochizuki were first into the castle, but in an act of carelessness uncharacteristic of ninja but no doubt helped by the pitch darkness, Arakawa fell into a pit. The moon had risen by the time Mochizuki pulled him to safety. Both men were dressed the same as the men of the garrison, and when the pine torches were rekindled they raced off through the middle of the enemy. To prove to their commander that they had got so far with their mission, they tore down one of the many banners bearing a Christian cross that fluttered everywhere in the castle, and took it back as a souvenir. As they descended the walls they were subjected to a hail of bullets, arrows and stones, which caused injuries from which they suffered for many days.

The long and patient blockade of the castle soon paid dividends. By the last few days of the siege, provisions were low, as the *Amakusa gunki* records:

White rice	10 koku
Soy beans	3 koku
Miso (fermented soy bean paste)	10 casks

As one koku was the theoretical amount needed to feed one man for one year, it can be seen how desperate their plight was becoming, and

A ninja fragmentation bomb in the form of the Chinese thunder crash bomb is shown in this picture from *Bansen Shukai*. The bombs had a metal case and worked by sending shards of the iron case far and wide. The illustration also shows how arquebus balls could be arranged inside the bomb. Noxious substances and jagged fragments of pottery could also be included to add to the mayhem.

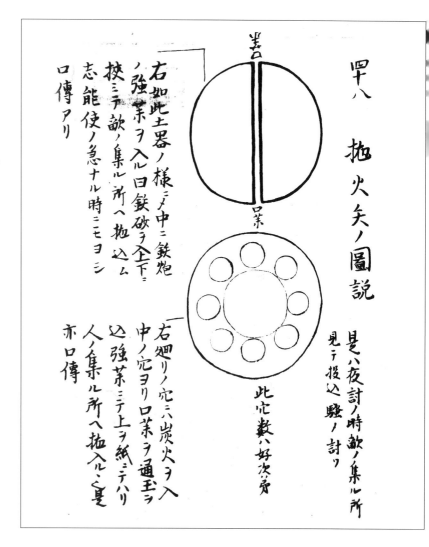

the garrison were reduced to eating the seaweed they were able to scrape off the rocks at low tide:

2nd month 20th day
A final counterattack that the enemy had planned was obstinately given back, but now the enemy army that attacked them had only seaweed and grass to eat.

2nd month 24th day
More and more general raids were begun, the Koga ninja band under the direct control of Matsudaira Nobutsuna captured the ni no maru and the san no maru, and after this, until the fall of the castle, they were under the command of Suzuki Sankuro Shigenari and his small ten-man unit, and Nakafusa Mino-no-kami, the head of the ninja 'office' sent from the Shogunate. They had a duty to communicate with the battle lines of each daimyo as they went into action.

The commander of Hara castle, Amakusa Shiro, tried a diversionary raid that, though brave, had little effect. It consisted of a disjointed charge into the besieging camps, and served largely to confirm in the Tokugawa soldiers' minds that the garrison were becoming very desperate indeed. When the final attack on Hara was launched, the Koga ninja acted in a liaison capacity between the various units assaulting the castle, as well as taking part in the actual fighting.

When Hara castle fell, it took with it the hopes of those who had led the Christian rebellion, and marked the last time that ninja would be used in battle. From this time on the operation of ninja would be theoretical rather than practical, with the myth growing stronger the further it diverged from reality.

AFTERMATH – THE NINJA MYTH

The tradition of making the ninja considerably larger than life has a very long history indeed. The first trend one can discern is that of associating ninja and ninjutsu with famous warriors who are historical personages, but who at some time in their careers led a mysterious or fugitive life. The two great heroes Minamoto Yoshitsune (1159–89) and Kusunoki Masashige (1294–1336) are the ones most often mentioned, to the extent that they are sometimes credited in popular works with the foundation of two separate 'schools of ninjutsu', the Yoshitsune-ryu and the Kusunoki-ryu, but there is no historical evidence whatsoever for either claim. In the case of Yoshitsune, identification is often made of his retainer, Ise Saburo Yoshimori, a samurai who accompanied him on his wanderings, as a skilled ninja, but in works such as the *Gikeiki* he is simply a loyal samurai warrior.

A ninja with the wall of Iga Ueno castle behind him.

The second identifiable trend is to link the ninja with the followers of Shugendo, the colourful yamabushi. On the face of things ninja and yamabushi seem to have little in common apart from their inherent mystery. Perhaps one reason may be that the guise of a wandering yamabushi was the ideal cover for a ninja in a role that involved espionage and travel. One of the greatest legends of Japan, that of Benkei and Yoshitsune's flight from Yoritomo, has ninja disguised as yamabushi, and there is a famous story about the barrier of Ataka, where the fugitives are challenged about their real identity. It is possible that yamabushi themselves acted as spies for rival daimyo, thereby abusing their right of free travel.

The final development of the ninja myth involved these undoubtedly authentic assassins and spies being transformed into superheroes. What is remarkable in this trend is that the process began while real ninja still had the potential to carry out their craft. Perhaps some of the operations they undertook, such as the murder of Uesugi Kenshin, seemed so inexplicable that the use of magic or invisibility was the only reasonable conclusion to draw. However, there are parallels with another transformation that was taking place at the same time: the creation of the myth of the invincible samurai swordsman. Just as the hardened battlefield warrior acquired a new image of the supreme individual samurai, so his unglam-orous and deadly mirror image that was the ninja acquired his own mysterious powers that transcended reality.

Two ninja on the wall of Iga Ueno castle.

In the pages above I have tried to paint as accurate a picture as I can of the elusive ninja. What have we learned about him? He was, first of all, a highly skilled fighter and martial artist who did not regard it as beneath his contempt to fight for money and to fight in ways that were officially socially unacceptable. He is likely to have belonged to one of a number of families that passed on their ninja traditions in great secrecy, as much to preserve their selling power as to maintain a purity of style. When he went into action he was prepared and willing to die, and would put into oper-ation extraordinary feats of self-endurance while he waited for the moment to strike.

Ninja fought in ways that samurai would not enter-tain and in situations and conditions where even the bravest samurai would hesitate to enter. With the authentic historical oper-ations noted above to consider, the greatest won-der is that anyone should feel it was necessary to create fiction out of ninja, when the facts concerning these most remarkable warriors of feudal Japan are themselves so extraordinary.

MUSEUMS, COLLECTIONS AND RE-ENACTMENT

My previous book, *Ninja: The True Story of Japan's Secret Warrior Cult* (Firebird, 1991), dealt only briefly with the places in Japan associated with ninja that one can visit today. In the intervening years I have been able to revisit these sites and also examine several others, and my impression of them is on the whole very positive. There are several places in Japan where the ninja's tourist potential has been very well realised, but be sure to check with the local tourist office before making any plans to visit.

The centre of the popularisation of ninja in Japan is undoubtedly Iga-Ueno in Mie Prefecture. The park in the castle grounds boasts a ninja house and a ninja museum. The house, moved from a nearby village and rebuilt, is very convincing. It contains several trap doors and concealed entrances, which are demonstrated to the visitor by two fetching young lady ninja, dressed in all-concealing ninja costumes, the effect of which is spoiled by the choice of bright pink or purple as a colour. The museum is also very interesting. The best time to visit Iga-Ueno is on the day early in April each year when the annual ninja festival is held. Events vary from year to year, and may include a parade and demonstrations by the local re-enactment society, who put on a very good show.

Koga, the rival to Iga in its supply of shinobi mercenaries, boasts two ninja tourist attractions. One is a ninja house very similar to the Iga version. The other is a preserved ninja village, complete with temple and shrine. Both are well worth visiting, but are not quite as accessible as the Iga sites.

Nijo jinya, the house in Kyoto used for the hypothetical assassination attempt related earlier, is well worth a visit. All the features noted in the fictional account actually exist in the house. Also worth seeing are all the fire precautions that enabled Nijo jinya to survive the Great Temmei Fire of 1788. A visit can be combined with nearby Nijo castle, where the sound of the famous 'nightingale floor' accompanies the visitor round the spectacular palace.

A further example of authenticity is found in the Teramachi district of Kanazawa. The Myoryuji was one of a number of temples relocated to the outskirts of the city by the third daimyo, Maeda Toshitsune, to provide an outer defence for Kanazawa. The Myoryuji possesses a number of secret rooms, concealed doors and secret passages, and is now inevitably known as 'Ninja-dera' or the 'ninja temple'. It is not the less worth visiting for that, because like Nijo jinya all the features are original.

A ninja on the wall of Iga Ueno. The stone bases of Japanese castles were very easy to climb because of the slope and the numerous hand holds.

Near Nagano is the location of the former Togakure-ryu school of ninjutsu. There is a ninja museum with a number of interesting displays, but nearby is a more popular attraction – a ninja theme park for children, where the accent is on having fun. A hire car is advised for these sites. Ninja also feature in the Ise Sengoku Jidai Mura, the 'samurai theme park', where various ninja acrobatic activities formed part of one of the regular displays when I visited in 1999. I must also confess to rather enjoying the ninja fun house!

Finally, it is possible to visit a genuine ninja's grave without leaving Tokyo, because the famous Hattori Hanzo is buried in the garden of the Seinenji temple, which lies near to Sophia University in Chiyoda-ku. Inside the temple hall is Hanzo's spear.

A ninja escapes in a hail of arrows from Hara castle in Shimabara in 1638 after his espionage mission. The siege of Hara provides some of the best authenticated accounts of ninja in action during the time of war. During one raid they captured some flags, which boosted the besiegers' morale.

GLOSSARY

Ashigaru	Foot soldier.
Chunin	Ninja 'officers'.
Daimyo	Feudal lord.
Futon	Folding mattress.
Genin	Ordinary ninja.
-gumi (kumi)	Military unit.
Gunkimono	War tale.
Hamagari	A long, thin folding saw.
Hara kiri	Ritual suicide.
Kancho	Spies.
Koku	A measure of rice, often also used to indicate wealth.
Komuso	A flute-playing Zen mendicant.
Koran	Agitators or disrupters.
Kunai	Implement for gouging holes in walls.
Maru	A castle's baileys. (ichi, ni, san means 1st, 2nd, 3rd)
Ninjutsu	Ninja techniques.
Sensei	Master or teacher.
Shinobi	Alternative reading of 'nin' in ninja.
Shinobigama	Ninja sickle and chain weapon.
Shogun	Military dictator.
Shonin	Ninja leader or headman.
-shu	Military unit.
Shugo	Provincial governor.
Shuriken	Throwing star.
Teisatsu	Scouts.
Yamabushi	Mountain ascetic.
Yashiki	Mansion.

Two members of the Iga Ueno ninja re-enactment group are about to enter the castle through its 'stone-dropping hole', the Japanese equivalent of machicolations. These holes would have a door across, secured from the inside, so the ninja would have to use cutting devices.

BIBLIOGRAPHY AND FURTHER READING

The reader who desires to know more about the historical reality of the ninja is recommended to read my earlier book, *Ninja: The True Story of Japan's Secret Warrior Cult* (Firebird, 1991). This work also contains an extensive bibliography, listing all the primary sources in Japanese quoted above.

For someone skilled in the Japanese language, I can wholeheartedly recommend *Ninja*, by various authors, in the series *Rekishi Gurafiko*, published by Shufu to Seikatsusha (Tokyo, 1993). This contains much information not available to me when I wrote my first book and has proved very useful for this present volume. There are a huge number of popular works on the market dealing with ninja fighting arts and ninjutsu. I do not feel qualified to comment on their accuracy or authenticity, but I note that works by Stephen Hayes are well regarded.

For more general works on the samurai and ninja see my books such as *Samurai Warfare* (Cassells, 1996) or *The Samurai Sourcebook* (Cassells, 1998). Details of the operation of Chinese explosive devices may be found in my *Siege Weapons of the Far East, Volume 1 and 2* in the Osprey New Vanguard series (2001 and 2002). Please visit my regularly updated website at **www.stephenturnbull.com** for announcements of new developments.

The Koga ninja house, viewed from outside the entrance courtyard. This was moved to its present site from a nearby village.

59

COLOUR PLATE COMMENTARY

A: NINJA IN TRADITIONAL COSTUME WITH ESSENTIAL PERSONAL EQUIPMENT

This plate shows a typical ninja figure in his traditional costume with the usual equipment that would be found about his person. The ninja costume is completely black, but, as is explained in the text, there were occasions when the ninja would wish to disguise himself, or simply dress up as one of an enemy castle's guards.

1. The costume itself is shown being worn by the central figure, while its component parts are shown separately below. The ninja suit was a simple but very well-designed item based around trousers and a jacket (11) that was not unlike the jacket worn for judo or karate. It has no ties, but so that nothing would catch on any protrusions when climbing a wall the 'tails' of the jacket were tucked inside the trousers, which were tapered and rather like the trousers commonly worn by samurai when riding a horse. They tied below the knee. Over the calves would be worn cloth gaiters, again very similar to standard samurai equipment, while on the feet would be black *tabi*, the classic Japanese socks with a separate compartment for the big toe and reinforced soles. *Waraji* (straw sandals) (10) would complete the ninja's footwear. A shirt with close-fitting arms also seems to have been worn according to most illustrations, and the whole ensemble was pulled tightly together round the waist by a long black belt. The ninja's head was wrapped in an all enveloping cowl, with only the face above the mouth, or even only the eye slits visible. His utility bag hangs from his belt.

2. *Tetsu bishi* (caltrops) could also be carried. These consisted of sharp iron spikes arranged in the shape of a tetrahedron so that one spike was always protruding upwards. As samurai wore thin-soled footwear, tetsu bishi could be very effective in slowing down pursuers.

3. We also see different shapes of *shuriken*, the 'ninja throwing stars' that were projected with a spinning motion.

In the inset boxes are the so-called 'ninja's essential six items'. They are as follows in a clockwise direction:

4. *Kaginawa* (hooked rope). This was the most important climbing device and would be carried from the ninja's belt when not in use.

5. *Amegasa* (sedge hat). A straw rain hat appears a most unlikely piece of ninja equipment, but it was commonly included among the 'six items' and would have been very useful for concealing one's identity as well as during the rainy season.

6. *Sanjaku tenugui* (three shaku (3-foot-long) towel), folded. This was the ninja equivalent of the samurai item that could be used as a bandage and a sling as well as a towel.

7. *Uchitake* (waterproof gunpowder container inside a bamboo tube). This was a simple powder flask doubly sealed against the weather. A tinderbox would be used for ignition. The purpose was more one of setting fire to something rather than creating an actual explosion.

8. *Inro* (medicine carrier). The inro was standard wear for any Japanese samurai, and consisted of a small lacquered box with several interlocking compartments, pulled tight by a draw cord. It could contain pills, potions and antidotes to poison.

9. *Seki hitsu* (literally 'stone brush'). A writing kit box with a slate pencil. Literacy was expected of a ninja so that he could draw a map of enemy installations and write messages. The box is lacquered to make it weatherproof.

B: NINJA SPECIALISED EQUIPMENT AND ITS USE

This plate shows various items of ninja specialised equipment in use.

1. *Kurorokagi* (a metal climbing device). This seemingly unnecessary piece of equipment consisted of a strong iron hook mounted on a wooden handle. Its purpose was to aid climbing, but as well as acting like an extension to the hand as shown here, it would probably also be very useful in providing a step for a descent. The insert diagram shows a similar iron climbing aid.

2. *Saoto hikigane* (listening device). The portable listening devices called saoto hikigane acted like an ear trumpet, so the ninja could listen in to conversations and ascertain the movements of guards. Details are shown in the insert diagram. They were essentially no more than simple tapered metal cylinders.

3. *Tsubokiri* (breaking and entering tool). Two devices in succession could open small gaps between the planking. The first was the tsubokiri, which looks like a two-pronged iron fork, which would enlarge the gap slightly by twisting, making a space just large enough for a thin leaf-shaped saw with small teeth to be inserted.

4. *Shikoro* (thin saw). Using this broad-bladed thin saw

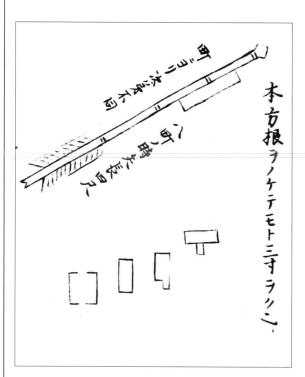

60 | *A ninja rocket from* Bansen Shukai.

a ninja could cut through wooden joints at the side of a window or an outside screen. The insert diagram shows a long-handled version.

5. *Kunai* (gouger). As Japanese castle walls were made on a wattle and daub core and plastered over, so a ninja would use a kunai, which looked like a cross between a broad-bladed knife and a paint scraper. By gouging and cutting, the ninja could rapidly carve out a hole large enough for him to climb through.

The interior of the Iga Ueno Ninja Museum, which was built as a basement floor to the Ninja House. Inside is a wide collection of ninja implements.

6. *Shinobi-gama* (sickle weapon). The sickle and chain combination was a well-known martial arts weapon that was derived from agricultural implements, and in its ordinary form was known as the *kusari-gama*. The chain had a weight on the end and could be flung to halt a pursuer. The attacker would then drag him off his feet and kill him with the sickle blade. The ninja version had a smaller but very sharp blade kept scabbarded when not in use.

7. *Hokode* (hand claws). These would help a ninja climb a wall and also act as an anti-personnel weapon in a fist fight.

8. *Tekagi* (claws or 'knuckle dusters'). These were made of iron and originated as wall-climbing devices. They could also be used for fighting.

C: NINJA DEVELOPMENT, TRAINING AND RECRUITMENT

This plate shows a boy ninja who is growing up in one of the ninja villages of Iga. By the time he has become a teenager he will be an expert in the basics of ninjutsu.

1. We see him first as a child learning the principles of balance under the watchful eye of his father, who will be his main trainer throughout his life.

2. Here our young ninja is learning how to breathe underwater using a bamboo breathing tube. One day this technique may save his life if he has to hide for hours under the surface of a lake to avoid pursuing enemies.

3. Sword practice is vital at every stage of a ninja's development. Here the young child gets his first lesson in how to be aware of assailants all around him. The enemies are just

branches hung from ropes, but the young ninja has to be able to anticipate how each will swing and how to avoid them.

4. The boy now undertakes extensive *shuriken* practice, learning how to spin the star-shaped missile and land it accurately against its target.

5. The young ninja learned survival skills the hard way by going off into the mountains and fending for himself. Here we see him cooking rice under a camp fire. The insert diagram shows how a handful of rice was wrapped in a cloth and soaked in water. The bag was buried under the fire to be cooked.

6. Here the young ninja is being interviewed by the *shonin* (the ninja leader in his village), who has been assessing his progress. When his training is complete he will be sent off on his first mission.

7. Very skilled and specialised teamwork skills are shown in these diagrams. Such well-practised acrobatic skills may well have given rise to the myths of ninja being able to fly. For example, there were two-, three- and four-man techniques for climbing over a wall. In the first type one ninja would run forward with his comrade on his shoulders, who would then leap from this elevated position.

8. Two men could assist a third to 'fly' over a wall by giving him a powerful 'leg up'.

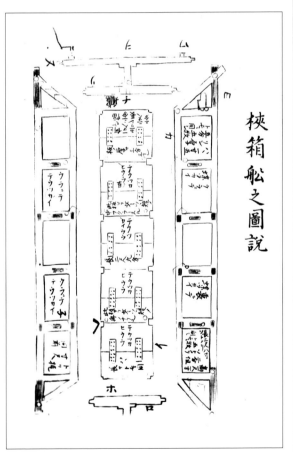

A prefabricated collapsible ninja boat from *Bansen Shukai*. The sections are fastened together using clamps, and surrounded by waterproofed cloth.

9. Four ninja might construct a human pyramid.

10. Here we see a ninja using the foot soldier's *yari* (pike-like long spear) and pole-vaulting over a gap.

D: A NINJA DISGUISED AS A YAMABUSHI RETURNS HOME TO HIS VILLAGE IN IGA PROVINCE

This plate shows a ninja returning home to his village in Iga Province after an undercover operation where he has been disguised as a follower of the Shugendo sect, commonly known as the *yamabushi*. Yamabushi wandered freely throughout Japan, so the role was perfect for a ninja engaged in spying.

In the foreground is the ninja dressed as a yamabushi. He is wearing the traditional costume of the pillbox hat and the white clothes with large pompoms, and is looking down into his village. The large *horagai* (conch shell trumpet) and *shakujo* (rattle) completes the illusion.

To an untutored eye the village in the valley is indistinguishable from any prosperous agricultural centre in a typical daimyo's territory, which is exactly what the villagers intend.

1. We notice a simple Buddhist temple with a graveyard and a Shinto shrine.

2. The big difference is in the means employed for the village's defence, but these are very subtle. On the hills around there are a series of smoke beacons to give advance notice of any attack, and a simple watchtower on the edge of the village.

3. Within the village itself the houses of the genin are located on the outskirts among the rice fields.

4. The home of the shonin is the village's central focus. This might look like nothing more than a wooden farmhouse such as would be occupied by any ordinary village headman, but it is located within a maze of rice fields which act as a moat when flooded, as they would be for much of the year. Steep earthen banks and a bamboo fence or prickly hedge provide other defences. The paths between the rice fields are narrow, and there are designated places where valuables may be buried.

E: A NINJA HOUSE

In this plate we are looking inside the shonin's house in the ninja village. It is every bit as well defended as the village. The house is a thatched farmhouse, but it is very cunningly designed. Many 'ninja' features have been added

The great ninja art of tying someone up, illustrated in step-by-step details from *Buke Senjin Saho Shusei* by Yoshihiko Sasama, reproduced here by kind permission of the publishers.

on to the basic-style Japanese farmhouse. These are intended as a defence against attack.

1. We see typical polished wooden corridors giving access to rooms floored with *tatami* (straw mats).

2. The shonin's main reception room is well guarded. There is a secret bolt hole behind the hanging scroll through which a guard can listen to the conversation and enter if required.

3. There is also a secret underground passage, and a very nasty booby trap in the corridor with spikes beneath. An assailant would not know which was which.

4. The upper floor is accessed by means of a 'rotating' staircase, pivoted so that it can snap shut.

5. The upstairs plaster walls are pierced with windows that can act as gunports.

6. The top storey is almost invisible, and has a trap door through the thatch leading to the roof.

F: NINJA ON CAMPAIGN 1: ENTERING A CASTLE

This plate shows a team of ninja engaged on one of their most characteristic activities – gaining access to a heavily defended castle to carry out espionage or assassination. In contrast to Plate H the emphasis here is on secrecy, before, during and after the operation. Here we see the first stage of the process, which involves crossing the castle moat and climbing up the stone walls.

The moat around the castle is filled with water and is too deep to wade through. The castle's walls are in the typical Japanese style of sloping surfaces made from stone. There are plenty of hand holds, but rope ladders are still useful, particularly for the uppermost sections. On one side we see a simple white plastered wall on top of the stone base, overhung by a pine tree, while on the other is an elaborate *tamon yagura*, a tower-like structure extending the length of the stone base. This allows only two means of entry, the stone-dropping hole and the heavily shuttered and barred window.

1. The ninja crossing the moat display three varieties of crossing equipment. The first uses *ukidaru*, two very clumsy bucket-like floats, which must have been unstable.

2. The second ninja is using a far more credible swimming aid, which consists of a series of floats tied together. This was a speciality of the Togakure-ryu of Nagano. The insert diagram shows them separated.

3. The third device being used is the famous wooden water spider that appears in *Banzen Shukai*. This was a speciality of the ninja of Koga.

4. The first ninja to begin climbing the wall is using a *shinobi kumade*, a collapsible sectioned bamboo pole that enables a hooked rope to be lifted over the branch of a tree with the minimum of sound.

5. This ninja shows how a sword could also be of use in climbing a wall, because the strong iron *tsuba* (sword-guard) could provide a step if the sword was leant against the wall. The ninja would loop the end of the suspensory cord round his foot so that he could pull his sword up when he had climbed the wall.

6. This ninja employs a rope ladder with a stout hook at the top. The rungs consist of a series of short bamboo sections. A rope was threaded through each section, alternating between pieces threaded across the middle and

through their whole length. A hook was attached to the top, and when the whole length of the rope was pulled tight and secured the result was a lightweight if flimsy ladder.

7. Shows how other help might be provided for the feet by *ashiko*, spiked climbing devices rather like crampons.

G: NINJA ON CAMPAIGN 2: ENTERING A DAIMYO'S MANSION FOR AN ASSASSINATION ATTEMPT

This is essentially a continuation of Plate F in that the ninja has now entered the daimyo's private apartments in the castle to assassinate him. These could be located inside the keep, which would make the ninja's task more difficult, but in many cases the *yashiki* (mansion) was a separate building within the inner bailey. The wall of the room is cut away so we can see the corridor and rooms. The interior design is typical of a daimyo's mansion. Within the heavy outside sliding doors there is a polished wooden corridor that leads to a succession of rooms divided from each other by paper screens. The floor of the corridor is a nightingale floor, and this may well have saved the daimyo's life.

1. A ninja has just entered the door using various 'burglar's tools' illustrated in Plate B. He is throwing ninja stars at the guards approaching down the corridor.

2. While his companion is dealing with the guards, a second ninja is killing the daimyo. The intended victim was asleep, but the sound of the nightingale floor awoke him, and he is now struggling with his assailant.

3. The insert diagram shows the ninja technique for exploring a potentially dangerous dark place such as a castle's corridors. The ninja would balance the sword's scabbard out in front on the tip of the sword blade, with the scabbard's suspensory cords gripped firmly between his teeth. This extended the ninja's range of feel by a good six feet, and if the scabbard end encountered an enemy, the ninja would let it fall and lunge forward in the precise direction of the assailant.

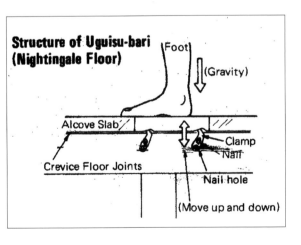

The mode of operation of the famous nightingale floor in Nijo castle in Kyoto. Contrary to popular belief, the squeaking sound is not produced directly by the floorboards themselves, but by the offset metal hinges triggered by the pressure of a foot. This is taken from the souvenir brochure of Nijo castle, by kind permission.

H: NINJA IN BATTLE: A CASTLE RAID DURING A SIEGE

Whereas the ninja in Plates F and G intended to enter, perform and leave in complete secrecy, the mode of operation depicted in this plate is somewhat different. It is just before dawn, and a group of ninja have climbed into a castle that is under siege. They have certain tasks to perform prior to the imminent dawn attack by the besieging army. We are looking down into the inner courtyard.

1. One ninja dressed identically to a guard is killing a guard. This makes the point that ninja did not always dress in black. The maximum confusion will be caused if the garrison cannot tell friend from foe.

2. Another ninja throws a small version of the Chinese-style hard-cased bombs, made either of pottery or iron. The latter could produce fearful wounds like a fragmentation bomb, and large models would have sufficient force to blow a hole in a castle's plaster walls. Small versions could be thrown by hand, making them effectively hand grenades. Ignition was provided from a tinderbox or a smouldering cord kept in a weatherproof lacquered container.

3. Another ninja kicks over the brazier that is the only source of illumination in the courtyard. Other ninja run about to cause mayhem in the castle. There is an explosion at the rear.

The ninja house at Iga Ueno, brought from a nearby village. This is one of the most popular sites on the ninja tourist trail.

INDEX

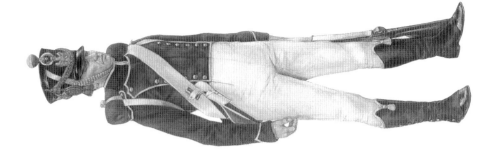

FIND OUT MORE ABOUT OSPREY

❏ Please send me the latest listing of Osprey's publications

❏ I would like to subscribe to Osprey's e-mail newsletter

Title / rank

Name

Address

City / county

Postcode / zip   state / country

e-mail

WAR

I am interested in:

❏ Ancient world
❏ Medieval world
❏ 16th century
❏ 17th century
❏ 18th century
❏ Napoleonic
❏ 19th century

❏ American Civil War
❏ World War 1
❏ World War 2
❏ Modern warfare
❏ Military aviation
❏ Naval warfare

Please send to:

USA & Canada:
Osprey Direct USA, c/o MBI Publishing, P.O. Box 1,
729 Prospect Avenue, Osceola, WI 54020

UK, Europe and rest of world:
Osprey Direct UK, P.O. Box 140, Wellingborough,
Northants, NN8 2FA, United Kingdom

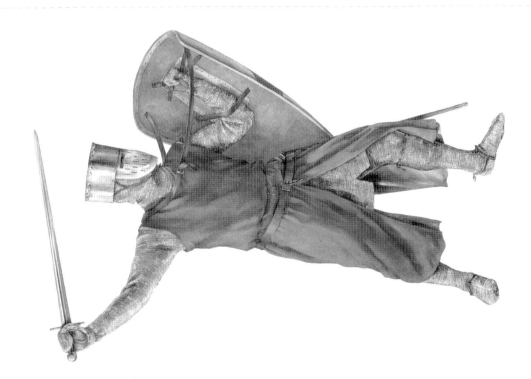

OSPREY
PUBLISHING

www.ospreypublishing.com

call our telephone hotline
for a free information pack

USA & Canada: 1-800-826-6600
UK, Europe and rest of world call:
+44 (0) 1933 443 863

Young Guardsman
Figure taken from *Warrior 22:
Imperial Guardsman 1799–1815*
Published by Osprey
Illustrated by Richard Hook

POSTCARD

Knight, c.1190
Figure taken from *Warrior 1: Norman Knight 950 – 1204 AD*
Published by Osprey
Illustrated by Christa Hook